CRITICAL VIEWS ON VICENTE ALEIXANDRE'S POETRY

VICENTE CABRERA and
HARRIET BOYER, Editors

CRITICAL VIEWS ON VICENTE ALEIXANDRE'S POETRY

SOCIETY OF SPANISH AND SPANISH-AMERICAN STUDIES

The Society of Spanish and Spanish-American Studies
promotes bibliographical, critical and pedagogical research
in Spanish and Spanish-American studies by publishing works
of particular merit in these areas.   On occasion, the Society
will also publish creative works.   SSSAS is a non-profit
educational organization sponsored by The University of
Nebraska-Lincoln.   It is located at the Department of Modern
Languages and Literatures, The University of Nebraska-
Lincoln, Oldfather Hall, Lincoln, Nebraska   68588, U. S. A.

SSSAS: HF-102 (LC)

International Standard Book Number (ISBN):   089295-006-4
Library of Congress Catalog Card Number: 79-65008

Printed in the United States of America
Impreso en los Estados Unidos de América

To Dámaso Alonso

TABLE OF CONTENTS

PROLOGUE

With this collection of essays the editors offer a comprehensive introduction to the vast, rich and complex world of Vicente Aleixandre. The book includes six major studies which focus on the development of Aleixandre's poetry from *Ambit* (1928) to *Dialogues of Knowledge* (1974) and delve into his major works and themes. The book also includes a general introduction, a selected bibliography, a biographical sketch and an English translation of the poems studied in the six essays and in the general introduction.* We would like to thank the authors for allowing us to incorporate their articles in this book and also for their help in the revision of the English version.

Spring of 1979.

Vicente Cabrera
Harriet Boyer
Colorado State University

* The Society of Spanish and Spanish-American Studies takes this opportunity to express its gratitude to Mr. Vicente Aleixandre for authorizing the publication of his poems.

ACKNOWLEDGMENTS

An earlier version of most essays included in this collection was published in the following periodicals:

Vicente Cabrera, «El *Mundo a Solas* de Aleixandre: Cosmovisión y metáfora del amor ausente,» *Journal of Spanish Studies: Twentieth Century,* Vol. 6, No. 2 (Fall 1978), pp. 77-96.

Guillermo Carnero, «'Conocer' y 'Saber' en *Poemas de la Consumación* y *Diálogos del Conocimiento,* de Vicente Aleixandre,» *Cuadernos Hispanoamericanos* No. 276 (June 1973), pp. 571-578.

Gene Forrest, «Vicente Aleixandre y Henri Rousseau: Una coincidencia en la imagen,» *Cuadernos Hispanoamericanos,* No. 301 (July 1975), pp. 115-120.

Ricardo Gullón, «Itinerario poético de Vicente Aleixandre,» *Papeles de Son Armandans,* Vol. II, No. 32-33 (November-December 1958), pp. 195-234.

José Olivio Jiménez, *Diez años de poesía española,* Madrid: Insula, 1972.

Kessel Schwartz, «The Isakower Phenomenon and the Dream Screen in the Early Poetry of Vicente Aleixandre,» *Revista de Letras,* Vol. 6, No. 22 (June 1974), pp. 210-218.

CHRONOLOGY

1898   Vicente Aleixandre was born in Sevilla on April 26th.
1900-1909   Lived in Malaga.
1909   Moved to Madrid, the place of his residence until the present. Entered the Colegio Teresiano.
1913   Graduated from high school.
1914   Entered the School of Law and Commerce.
1917   Met Dámaso Alonso who introduced Aleixandre to poetry through an anthology of Rubén Darío.
1920   Finished his studies in Law and Commerce.
1921   His interest in poetry increased. Read Bécquer, Góngora, Machado.
1924-1927   Started and completed his first book of poetry: *Ambit*. Became seriously ill and retired to the countryside at Miraflores de la Sierra.
1928   *Ambit* was published.
1928-1929   Wrote *Passion of the Earth*.
1930-1931   Wrote *Swords like Lips*.
1932   Became ill again and had his kidney removed.
1933   Wrote *Destruction or Love* and won the National Prize for Literature for this book.
1934   His mother died and he traveled through England and France. Started to write *World Alone*.
1935   *Passion of the Earth* was published.
1936   Completed *World Alone*.
1936-1939   Became ill once more.
1939   His father died.
1944   Published *Shadow of Paradise* which he started to write in 1939.
1945-1953   Wrote *History of the Heart* and published *Ultimate Birth* which he started in 1927.
1949   Was elected to the Royal Academy.
1950   *World Alone* was published.
1953   *Ultimate Birth* was published.

severity or art and creation with all its genuine *elán*».(2)   They believed in a pure poetry, a poetry free of elements that are not necessary for the exact expression of their inner perception.(3) They are convinced that form is beautiful not because of the special use of words that may or may not be more poetic than others -- in fact all words are potentially beautiful and poetic – but because within the unique context of the poem those words have enabled the poet to aptly materialize his inner world.   What is not needed to achieve this goal must be eliminated and discarded. Their poetic refinement derives not from a capricious exaltation of form but from a genuine necessity of expression.

As a whole, the group relied on metaphor as the main technical device for poetic composition.   But again, its use was inspired by and directed to the exact utterance of the poet's feelings and intuitions, and to the purification of his craft.   The emphasis on metaphor throughout each poet's career changed normally from a complex hermetic diction to a more open and almost direct language, depending always on what the poet felt was the most exact expression for the subject with which he was dealing at the time.   But form was never an end in itself, only a means.   Unlike the other schools of the period, such as Surrealism, this group of poets never took a stand against tradition. On the contrary, with great critical insight they went back to such poets as Berceo, Lope de Vega, Góngora, Bécquer, Darío, Unamuno, Jiménez and Machado.   They saw in these poets not only a luminous poetic integrity, but also the very substance of Spanish poetry itself.   Since they were in search of an essential type of art, they reacted, however, against the prosaism and mediocrity of some 19th century poets such as Campoamor and Núñez de Arce, just like they also reacted against the surrealist precept of automatic writing.   They did work of course with Surrealism and other avant-garde schools but only as long as these schools offered them more devices to reach an exact and perfect expression.   And it is precisely the combination of the traditional with the new that made, for example, Lorca's or Aleixandre's or Guillén's poetry what it is today: «art with all its severity of art and creation with all its genuine *elán*».   As Aleixandre said in his acceptance speech of the Nobel Prize: The two key words of his generation were tradition and revolution.(4)

Most of these poets were engaged not only in writing poetry but also in studying it.   And some of the finest studies on the subject have come from the pen of these poets. Of special note are the essays on poetry by Dámaso Alonso, Jorge Guillén, Pedro Salinas, Rafael Alberti and Luis Cernuda.

The initial reaction of critics towards the poetry of this group was mixed: On the one hand, there was an immediate enthusiam and joy and, on the other, a displeasure on perceiving a degree of dehumanization in their art. They felt that this poetry was exceedingly abstract, too intellectual and cold, overwhelmed by a frivolous formalism that suffocated its content. The attacks, however, became obsolete and have ultimately vanished with the appearance of new and more perceptive studies which have disclosed and explained, once and for all, the human substance and emotion that lie beneath the surface of this difficult and essential poetry. Because they strive to make the poem as poetic as possible, and strived to identify poetry with the poem as much as possible, their creations were free of sentimental, social or political themes. They delved, instead, into the depths of the human soul by dealing with universal themes such as: Love, Death, Time, and Reality.

II

Vicente Aleixandre

Vicente Aleixandre was born in the Andalusian city of Sevilla on April 26, 1898. In 1909, Madrid became the city of his permanent residence after having lived in Málaga with his family for a few years. His first exposure to literature, at the age of 15, came about through the Spanish novel of the 19th century (Galdós, Valera, and Alarcón) and the Spanish Golden Age theater, mainly Lope de Vega's. Poetry at this time was not only of no interest to the young Aleixandre, but avoided as well. But not for too long, for in 1917 he met Dámaso Alonso who gave him a poetic anthology of the great Modernist poet Rubén Darío and ever since his passion for poetry became, as the poet has indicated, the passion of his life. Immediately after this revelation, Aleixandre started to discover the work of other important Spanish poets: Antonio Machado, Juan Ramón Jiménez and Unamuno; and in 1920 he began writing his own verses which were

never published but some of which have been kept by his friend
Dámaso Alonso. His poetic curiosity expanded and became
part of his avid reading: Joyce, Rimbaud, Novalis, Keats,
Shelley and Wordsworth. In 1924, he began writing *Ambit*, his
first book of poetry, and at the same time became acquainted with
the other poets of the Generation of 1927. From 1924 on, his work
would grow almost uninterrupted despite serious health complications, as in 1932 when he had his kidney removed, and in 1936-
1939,during the Civil War. When in November of 1977 the Nobel
Prize was awarded to Vicente Aleixandre, the Swedish Academy
honored not only the poet, but also the generation to which he
belongs and the tradition from which he emerged.

III

Aleixandre's poetic world

    The poetic world of Vicente Aleixandre can be divided into
three major periods: 1) From *Ambit* to *Ultimate Birth,* 1928-
1953; 2) From *History of the Heart* to *Portraits with a Name,*
1954-1965; 3) From *Poems of Consumation* to *Dialogues of
Knowledge,* 1968-1974. Even though the three periods differ
from one another in form and content, they coherently develop
and structure one solid and complex poetic whole, nurtured and
permeated, as Carlos Bousoño indicates, by one key passion, that
of union and solidarity of man with the cosmos, and of man with
mankind, a union which constitutes the poet's self-realization and
fulfillment.(5)
1) *Cosmic solidarity.* Vicente Aleixandre conceives man as a
cosmic entity and, as such, his self-realization depends on his total
union, through love, with the universe. As a part or piece of the
universe, man is (or must be) in permanent harmony and solidarity
with the other elements of the cosmos. His destiny is to share
and enjoy it with all of them. The forest, the rock, the ocean,
the beetle, the sun, the tiger, the cloud and man are all participants of this cosmic communion, and are entities which appear
united in the poem as they are in the universe. The poet becomes
part of the universe and, through his word and art, the force which
unites the participants. The poem is the microcosm of the

universe itself. As the very focus and center of unification, the poet is the destiny of all the cosmic elements:

I am the destiny that summons all those who love,
sole sea to which all radiating lovers will come
who seek their center, curled by the circle
that whirls like the rose resounding and total.

I am the horse that inflames its mane against the bare wind,
I am the lion tortured by his own mane,
the gazelle that fears the indifferent river,
the conquering tiger that lays waste the jungle,
the tiny beetle that also shines in the day.

His identification with them is such that he relinquishes his own identity in order to become what they are, and this self-destruction is his own salvation and self-realization. In «Song to a Dead Girl» from *Destruction or Love* the poet says:

Tell me why on your loose hair,
on your sweet grass caressed,
there falls, slips, caresses and goes away
a sun burning or reposed that touches you
like a wind that carries only a bird or a hand.
...
Oh you, a song to a body dead or living,
to a beautiful being that sleeps under the soil,
you sing stone colored, kiss or lip colored,
you sing as if the nacre were sleeping or breathing.

Death is not death but life since the girl has reached her ultimate goal: to be an everlasting part of the universe. Death -- the cessation of the matter -- is the final step in the poet's cosmic reintegration since the matter, flesh, shall continue living in the matter, flesh, of the universe. Indeed, the poet generated with this cosmic vision, what critics called, a poetry of mystical pantheism.

In «Unity in Her», from *Destruction or Love,* the trilogy of Love, Death and Life is formed:

I want love or death, I want to die entirely,
I want to be you, your blood, that raging lava
that enclosed by nourishing beautiful extremities
feels thus the beautiful limits of life.

Death, Love and Life are synonymous. In the instinctive and erotic union of the lovers the three concepts become one: Life.

The passion with which he exalts the living entities of the universe is used in order to condemn and punish man's indifference to love and his refusal to be part of the cosmos; this is particularly true in *World Alone,* one of the most severe and painful books of Aleixandre's poetry. Towards the end of this period, in *Shadow of Paradise,* the poet perceives two visions: first, the cosmos before man's arrival, and second, man's transitory nature which establishes limitations and also anticipates the mood and themes of his second poetic world initiated with *History of the Heart.*

The restrictive form of the Spanish ballad -- *romance* -- widely used in *Ambit* could not control the exuberance and profusion of the cosmic vision of the poet, already evident in this early book and prevalent through *Ultimate Birth. Ambit,* for this reason, fails to be a successful work. Aleixandre's second experiment in search of a poetic diction that would hold the exhuberance of his cosmic vision is done through the turbulent, surrealist prose of *Passion of the Earth,* his second work, this time with more success. Neither extreme, however, was pleasing to Aleixandre, who instead, opted -- starting with *Swords like Lips* -- for a long, uninhibited verse structured with a constellation of irrational and visionary images, that would create the distinctive Aleixandrine poetic diction of the first phase.(6) Of these two stylistic extremes (of *Ambit* and of *Passion of the Earth*), it is from the second that Aleixandre would extract the light of his poetry. From the chaotic darkness of the tormented and subconscious world of *Passion of the Earth* will progressively rise the luminous reality of *Shadow of Paradise,* the book which, along with *Destruction or Love* and *History of the Heart,* would later become perhaps the most influential work in contemporary Spanish literature.

2) *Human solidarity.* If the cosmos was the central theme of the first phase, of the second, is man: man in relation to time and limited by it, and man in relation to love and, therefore, able to forge a solidarity of peaceful coexistence among men. Just as in the previous period Aleixandre sought the fusion of man with

nature, now he promotes the fusion of man with man through love. In «The Poet Sings for Everyone», from *History of the Heart*, the most representative book of this period, the poet joins the people—men, women, and children — to create one single entity. His destiny and salvation is to transform the beating of his own heart into that of the people, into that of humanity, in order to sing the only song, the song of mankind:

And for all ears.   Yes.   Look how they hear you.
They are listening to themselves.   They are listening to   a
single voice that sings them.
The very mass of the song, they move like a wave.
And you submerged, almost dissolved, like a knot of their
being you know yourself,
The voice that carries them sounds.   It lies down like a road.
All feet are treading on it.
They are treading on it beautifully, they are engraving it
with their flesh.
And it unfolds and offers, and the whole mass gravely files on.
Like a mountain it climbs.   It is the path of those who march.
And it ascends to the clear peak.   And the sun opens up on
their foreheads.
And at the peak, with its grandeur, everyone is now singing.
And it is your voice that expresses them...

Not only is the poet the leader, but also, and most important, he is the very self of the others who form the community of men.

Since he cannot remain static or immobile in his view of man, he moves from man's childhood to adolescence, to maturity, to old age and finally to death.   But not to despair over it but to serenely accept death as another manifestation of life:

We two have slowly looked at each other.
How mamy times you tell me: «Don't remind me of the
years»
But you also tell me, at times of closeness and whispering:
«Yes, the years are you, are your love.   We exist»
Now that nothing changes, that nothing can change, like life
itself, like me, like together...
Slow growing of the branch, slow curving, slow extending: slow,
at last, far away, slow bending.   And branch filled with fruit,

> *so laden, so rich*
> *so continously together: like a gift, like being here--*
> *until another hand that may be, that will be, picks it,*
> *more still than like the earth, like love, like a kiss.*

(From «We Won't Die» of *History of the Heart*)

Due to his concept of solidarity the poet feels the necessity to write to and for everyone:

> *I write perhaps for the ones who don't read me.   That woman who runs down the street as if she were opening doors for the dawn.*
>
> *Or that old man who drowses on the bench in that small plaza, while the setting sun with love takes him, surrounds him and softly dissolves him in its lights.*
>
> *For all those who don't read me, those who don't care about me, but care about me (although they may be unaware of me).*
>
> *That little girl who as she passes looks at me, companion of my adventure living in the world...*

(From «For Whom I Write» of In a Vast Dominion)

What he says here agrees with what Aleixandre always had said about his poetry as being communication and comunion with life.(7)

Unlike his first phase, where his poetic diction was determined by a complex and intricate metaphoric composition and development, his verses now acquire a more direct and open expression, a more transparent linguistic pattern, allowing a direct dialogue with the reader who needs not be an expert in poetic interpretation in order to receive the message from the poet. Its originality depends not on the novelty of the imagery, but on the lucid and tender manipulation of a common language that utters a deeply felt identification with his fellow men, with their hopes and limitations.   Such is his conviction that the poet is humanity and vice versa.   And in this union ultimately rests the self-realization of Aleixandre as a man and as a poet. This new thematic vision is in no way a departure from his previous one but, rather, its consequence and its complement. After all, it is the same solidarity which opens itself in two mutually dependent directions: Man and the Universe.

With the publication of *In A Vast Dominion* Aleixandre reaches a marvelous synthesis of the two phases by returning to the cosmic matter and turning it into life, and life into history. Man is the result of the long evolution of cosmic matter, a matter which, never static, patiently has become a leg, a sex organ, an arm, a hand, a stomach, a chest, a head and the Spirit of man. And if in some cases, the matter has not developed normally, the poet shall identify himself with the physically and mentally abnormal, for they are also part of the loving community of man.

3) *Solidarity of the Spirit.* Two books form this third phase: *Poems of Consumation* and *Dialogues of Knowledge*. In an introspective and meditative mood, the poet attempts to deal with major concepts such as Life, Death and Time. It is the metaphysical period of the poet who, in his old age, with wisdom, looks back at his life in an attempt to grasp the meaning of those concepts. But he finds that such an endeavor reaches more than a certainty, a doubt, a doubt which asserts the existence of man. In *Poems of Consumation* this doubt reaches pessimistic proportions since the wisdom of the old poet only evinces the certainty of death. In *Dialogues of Knowledge*, as Aleixandre has indicated: «each character [of the dialogue] says 'something' about reality, perhaps, contrary to what the other asserts, but no less true. The richness of the world can only be talked about from a multiple perspective».(8) The originality of the book, and perhaps its whole secret, rests on the confrontation of the two points of view which never reach a solution and leave the subject in the same state of mystery and ambiguity as before the poem was started. And the reader is left in a deeper confusion and frustration, but also illuminated by the fact that reality is what it is not. Furthermore, within the reasoning of each dialogist arise contrasting perceptions and feelings about the subject they confront. This is why the book becomes a poetic illusion of reality, as will be demostrated later, in the study of the conjunction «or». In both books contradiction is the essence of content and form.

The intimate connection of the two books makes the third

phase a single and unified poetic experience. And, to strenghten this unity, Aleixandre creates a textual dialogue between the two books. Almost entire verses from the first book reappear in the second book. Furthermore, this textual dialogue also connects this third period with the other two previously studied. Such is the case when the line: «I knew what love was because I lived daily» (of «Form without Love» from *World Alone*) reappears, almost entirely, in «The Old Lovers» from *Dialogues of Knowledge: «I knew what it is to love because I lived daily.»* But this intertextual dialogue, more than a rectification, is an expansion in order to proliferate the perspectives of reality.

Unlike the linguistic pattern of the two other phases, in the last one Aleixandre introduces a new form which is, in general, short, irregular, and never smooth, yet appropriate to capture the brusque mobility of the intellect. At times, the surrealist complexity of the earlier works is used again to intensify the complexity of the intricate formulas of the intellect in *Poems of Consumation* and *Dialogues of Knowledge.* Also the typical Aleixandrine use of the conjunction «or», prevalent in the first phase, reappears in the third one with a double function: a)   to identify two different concepts as equal in meaning (death or life means death is life. This was the only function of the «or» in *Destruction or Love*) and b)   to intensify the ambiguity of the individual's perception of reality, since the two concepts offer different alternatives which confuse the protagonist 's situation. In the poem «The Young Lovers» from *Dialogues of Knowledge,* he, at the end of his dialogue with her, strikes down the walls that have impeded him from reaching her. He says: «...there has opened/ the garden of life, or the earth, or death». Here, the garden and life are the same, so are the earth and death. But the garden and earth, and life and death are not the same, yet paradoxically they are. He does not know exactly whether what he finds behind the walls is life of death, garden or earth. Nor does he know if what he finds is life which is also death. In Aleixandre's first phase the «or» never originated this type of ambiguity since it merely identifiedas equal two different concepts, but here, in his last two books, the «or» is both an inclusive and exclusive particle.

Each phase of Vicente Aleixandre's poetry, as was stated at

the beginning of this study, has a coherent thematic development and its own poetic diction, appropriate to the nature of the content it expresses. But with the same intensity and spirit they differ from each other, they also expand and enrich on single and unified poetic and metaphysical world which opens itself in three different and complementary directions: the Universe, Man and his Spirit.

NOTES

1. It is called the Generation of the Dictatorship because the first poetic appearance of most of its members coincided with the dictatorship of Primo de Rivera, from 1923-1931.

2. Jorge Guillén, *Language and Poetry. Some Poets of Spain.* (Cambridge: Harvard University Press, 1961), p. 204.

3. Guillén insists on the fact that «all of them strove for the most exact expression.» Guillén, *Language and Poetry,* p. 204.

4. Vicente Aleixandre, «Discurso de recepción del Premio Nobel», *Insula,* No. 378 (May 1978), p. 1.

5. Carlos Bousoño, *La poesía de Vicente Aleixandre,* 3ª ed. (Madrid: Gredos, 1968), pp. 45-46. This book is by far the most comprehensive study of Aleixandre's poetic world. The only two books of poetry which are not considered in Bousoño's study are *Poems of Consummation* and *Dialogues of Knowledge.*

6. For the study of this visionary imagery, see Carlos Bousoño's book, *La poesía de Vicente Aleixandre,* pp. 147-208.

7. See his essay, «Poesía comunicación», in his *Obras Completas* (Madrid: Aguilar, 1966), pp. 1581-1583.

8. Quoted by Darío Puccini in his article, «Hacia una tipología de la contradicción: Vicente Aleixandre: *Diálogos del conocimiento*» *Papeles de Son Armadans,* No. 81 (April 1976), p. 26.

A POETIC ITINERARY

Ricardo Gullón
The University of Chicago

From clarity into the shadow

Vicente Aleixandre came to poetry a little later than the others of his group. We know, from the poet's own statements, how he discovered poetry: in a village in the Sierra of Avila, when he was eighteen, he met Dámaso Alonso, who was to become his close friend, and Alonso lent him a book of Rubén Darío's poetry. This was the first book of this kind to fall into Aleixandre's hands, and he says: «That truly virginal reading was a revolution to my spirit. I discovered poetry: it was revealed to me, and then began the great passion of my life which was never to be diminished.»(1)

Shortly thereafter he fell ill and the illness, forcing him to seek rest and solitude for several years, made him concentrate on reading and on poetic creation. In 1928, he published his first book, *Ambit*, in the lovely Málaga edition from *Litoral* which also published Cernuda's first collection *Perfil del Aire* and works by Prados, Lorca and Moreno Villa, among others. *Ambit* is a collection of candid nostalgia; a small adolescent book clear in language and feeling with nothing revolutionary or even daring.

In this same year, 1928, a radical transformation occurred in Aleixandre's poetry; while the moderate *Ambit* was being published, he was writing the prose poems which would be published in 1935 in Mexico with the title *Passion of the Earth*. These poems revealed a different perspective on man and different talents of the poet. With these prose poems and other poems from *Swords like Lips* written shortly afterwards, Aleixandre attempted to capture more confused and turbid areas of the world and movements of the soul than in his first book. He went beyond moderation and limited lyrical ambition to a will to reveal dark, formless, almost inapprehensible presences of the subconscious.

There is a rupture between *Ambit* and *Passion of the Earth* (or *Swords like Lips*). And something more important: a new awareness of things, problems and situations not expressed in the first collection; the discovery of another universe latent beneath or beyond the visible. As a novice poet, it had been sufficient for Aleixandre to capture the graceful skater gliding across the ice, or the nocturnal landscape, to identify with the night, to feel a sense of poetry. This was not enough. From 1928 on, he comes into contact with other realities, or ultrarealities, and he concentrates his effort on expressing these as he intuits them.

The quality of these intuitions, as Carlos Bousoño has demonstrated in his penetrating study,(2) is unmistakably vision-ary. Aleixandre senses the world with his eyes open and life appears to him an ongoing parade of shadows which he tries to identify; but holding always to the plane of the visual rather than to that of a risky possible interpretation of it, he describes it as it presents itself to him or, more accurately, as he intuits it. This is the time when Aleixandre's poetry could most properly be called «surrealist,» since in *Passion of the Earth* (and in *Swords like Lips*) we find at least one of the conditions for this type of creation: Immersion in the world of the irrational without any previous logical supports.

As I have said elsewhere with regard to similar stages in Lorca and Cernuda, when one speaks of surrealism in Spanish poetry, it is necessary to understand it as a heterodox surrealism which never accepts the abdication of artistic consciousness although, as happens in these books by Aleixandre, the poet might seem from time to time to let himself be dragged along by impulses from the subconscious. There is no contradiction in this. The poet recognizes the reality of certain presences intuited in dreams, or more frequently in fantasies, and he wants to present them in their own truth which is usually topsy-turvy. But with the inevitability derived from necessity, the word is ordered despite itself in the expressive system which reflects the complete being of the creator (including, of course, consciousness): tne image of the visionary together with the vision.

Descent into the Abyss

What a splendid lesson there is in *Passion of the Earth,* a youthful, rich, overflowing book of dazzling darkness! A lesson for soulless rhetoricians, for they will find another world revealed, decisively penetrated by the poet, searching in the shadows, feeling around in the presence of the discovery of forms where the diverse elements of this very order take shape. Aleixandre was facing a very difficult problem: to give personal expression to poetic subjects situated on the farthest edge of the real and even beyond. To resolve this adequately, he had to plunge into the abyss and, probingly, gather in the objects within his reach. In this connection, we must not forget that the original title of *Passion of the Earth* was *Evasion toward the Depths.*
It is, therefore, not surprising that these poems comprise an extremely varied combination of intuitions, a combination which tends to be ordered around the essential themes.

But I am not sure whether, when I write «themes» in the plural, I commit an error. The personal interpretation of the poet and a careful examination of the book show the impossibility of separating out «themes» or subjects in these compositions. Even using the term «subject» in its loosest sense as equivalent to «theme» (love, death, etc.), it is noticeable that in *Passion of the Earth* everything is mixed and purposely indiscriminate. For an intelligent poet, which Aleixandre is, it would not have been difficult to create a fictitious or simulated order, but to do that, he would have had to renounce two essential qualities: the personal note and authenticity. To opt for the harsh path of unlimited effort and painful search—with the constant risk of failure—was aesthetically necessary. This is why this book was composed with its dark, dense palpitation.

Man lives in darkness and to find the road to light he lets himself be guided by instinct. Aleixandre did not seek clarity by following previously trodden paths; by submerging himself in the realm of the subconscious, in the realm of that hidden reality that exerts a powerful influence over the life of man, he sought to capture the living chaotic course of determinations which, without the acquiescence of the conscious self, affect behavior and feeling and give them their spice and flavor. This may correspond with the tenets of surrealism or super-realism but it really represents an effort to penetrate regions of the soul different from the ones already known and governed by reason. As is evident in *Passion of the Earth,* he returned from this adventure enriched, like one who comes back to the ordinary after visiting hell, a spiritual hell where contraries are joined and the opposition between the real and the fantastic has been resolved.

Already at this early stage which will culminate in *Shadow of Paradise,* the powerful lyrical energy of Aleixandre moves him to create a vast and complex universe where objects are used to emphasize the fundamental solitude of man. The certainty of this solitude makes up the profundity of *Passion of the Earth* and infuses it with an impassioned tone which stands out sharply beneath, or beyond, its eventual significance. There is something in the feeling of solitude that moves us because it reveals a slightly veiled despair due to the wretchedness and inanity of man. Thanks to some of Aleixandre's more recent poems (especially «It Is Not Enough,» the last poem in *Shadow of Paradise,* which is understood as an affirmation of faith and as the expression of the need for a God beyond the signs of his presence in the beauty of the earth), the intention of these early poems can be understood when it is seen that in the poet's despair there was a germ of hope almost imperceptible at that time.

In *Passion of the Earth*, chaos is still chaos and the poet's anguish is real and painful. He knows that his message does not communicate an agreeable present but rather an inexorable and bitter *memento mori.* It was not easy to express the turbulent flood boiling in his spirit; a flood of earthly things, too human at times, which produced an impassioned, impure poetry paradoxically full of brilliance.

Perhaps because of suggestions in Dámaso Alonso's essay on *Swords like Lips* or perhaps because of one of Aleixandre's poems, this poetry inspires in me feelings which I associate with Ravel's *La valse.* The themes indicate, arise from, and fade into a sonorous mist, and from time to time, they break through it. Similarly the rhythm of the prose poems of *Passion of the Earth* is a rising tide. The poet has felt life as a petty place, a sordid waiting-room where we wait for death to signal our turn and to force us to cross to the other side, as described in «Death or the Waiting Room»:

They were coming in one by one and the bloodless walls were not made of cold marble. Innumerable, they entered and greeted each other with their hats. Short-sighted demons visited their hearts. They looked at each other without confidence. Tags lay all over the ground and the wasps ignored them. A taste of dry earth suddenly exploded on their tongues and they spoke of everything with knowledge. That woman, that lady argued with her hat and very slowly everyone's chest caved in. Waters. Shipwreck. Steady glances. The sky stayed in its place and smoke from far-off touched everything. The fingers of the hand of the oldest man were so sad that the hallway slowly came closer, drifting, loaded with stories. Everyone turned wholly within and a curtain of smoke became blood. Without being able to help it, the shirts trembled under the coats and the labels became embroidered on flesh. 'Tell me, do you love me?' The youngest girl smiled full of promise. Breezes, breezes from below dispelled all the mist, and she was nude, colored with accents, pure prosody. 'Yes, I love you'--and the walls full of condensation almost evaporated.(3)

It is easy to separate the decisive images in this prose poem from the incidental allusions. Men are combining their desolation, their anguish. There is the fearlessness of the grand lady whose imposing presence seems to overwhelm all those around her. And there is also love in the couple voluntarily blind to everything else, closing their eyes in order to hold on to their precarious idea and prevent the fires of reality from entering their souls. The lovers are the only ones who for a moment manage to isolate themselves, but in the end they, like the others, will feel overcome by the call which will end the episode like the dull roll of the drum.

Aleixandre speaks of anguish. I prefer to call this feeling despair; the same kind of despair, according to Kierkegaard, which arises from the desire to be oneself, not a hidden despair but open and consequently susceptible to remedy and cure. In other poems, this feeling reveals more sinuous aspects. In

«Clothing and Serpent,» the desperate man despairs because of his own illusion and he tries to cast off the external and the adventitious in order to find himself naked, not for the sake of changing but to be totally unhampered by clothing which debilitates and subjugates:

> *One by one, all of the wrappings of my life will fall.*
> *Long serpent! Come forth. Surround the world.*
> *Emerge. Horrible python, be me so I can be in you.*
> *So I can, by surrounding myself, stretch, suffocate,*
> *undo myself. I shall emerge from my cadaver lifting*
> *my coils, as large as all articulated purposes, slithering*
> *across my own abandoned history and all the birds*
> *that came out of my desires, all the blue, pink, white,*
> *tender palpitations that sang in my ears will return to*
> *my jowls and will flash with liquid brilliance through my*
> *green glances. Oh unique night! Oh robust body*
> *which you raise up like a giant whip and with the sharp*
> *tooth of perfidy you strike the flesh of the early m oon.*(4)

The memories, the past, all previous experience. . . , all this he would like to lose in return for the authenticity raised up in the unique night of transformation which he suspects is magnificent. It is a dream reflected in a slowly developed image, a slowness which exhausts the theme. The idea is expressed as a direct presentation through images. There are no concepts in this poetry, only images. Images on different levels: the real and the imaginary. The fusion of the two, effected without continuity, gives rise to difficulties in interpretation; the breaks in logical inference cause confusion in the reader. The poet's voice indicates no transition: in referring to these two levels, he is equally mysterious in his efforts to discover unknown worlds without limits; at the same time, he sings of man's pain, of his permanent, secret anguish to attain barely formulable limbos, of his awareness that he is rooted in the earth as in his own element, waiting for death.

It is useless to think that these poems for the initiated will reveal their secret on the first reading. it is necessary to go back over them, to persist, and each time they will give up a part of their mystery, a metaphor will become clearer, we will notice the resonance of a word. At first, it will be certain chords wrapped in mist as in *La valse*; slowly the motifs will emerge and only after much reading will we fully apprehend the full meaning. But al least for me, certain fragments of *Passion of the Earth* are so hermetic that their meaning remains inaccessible Aleixandre's rejection and repudiation of previous and contemporary lyrical tradition is complete; he seeks the salvation of his poetic self in the dark and the impure. At times there is incoherence, but it inspires in the reader the timorous attitude of one who fears being duped or mystified.

What saves Aleixandre is the sincerity with which he tries to present to us his world in its integrity as well as the powerful spirit of his verse. In *Passion of the Earth,* he reveals his desire to transcend, to attain the limits of the unknown by means of poetry; poetry is the means to discover the ultimate secrets of man and of the universe. If the universe lacks meaning, poetry discovers this lack and the poem reflects this tremendous discovery. In «The World Is Well Made,» beings like Kafka's hasten to escape their destiny: they contemplate the night above the woods, they feel love nearby and dangers close. They want to flee and can't; they still fear and they still trust. Driven by haste, they run. But:

> *If we have already arrived, you must be seeing how the whitewashed wall has turned into lava, into the instantaneous siren of 'Tell me, tell me so I can answer you'; of 'Love me so I can show you'; of 'Submerge and you will learn how to give light like the moon' in the form of the silence that kisses the steppe of the great dream. 'Love me' the cricket chirp. 'Love me' the unsheathed cactuses call out. 'Die, die' ponders the great, long, cold serpent who looms in the divine eye and finds that the world is well made.(5)*

They have come to the moment when the ordinary collapses. The whitewashed wall signifies the house, the very circle of life, and its transformation into lava expresses through an image of great plasticity not only the collapse of the place where that existence has occurred, but also its conversion into an avalanche of matter pushed by demonic forces which tear everything down. And in the great dream there are voices which invite us to die in order to know, while on earth the song of existence calls us to live. But it will be death, the great serpent, who triumphs, satisfied with this creation entirely within her power.

Swords like Lips

In the third book by Aleixandre, we stay in the dark, acrid universe of *Passion of the Earth*, but I find a beginning of order and a spark of hope. The ascent toward the light is beginning. If the salient image of the earlier work is death, in *Swords like Lips* it begins to be love, life, prefiguring the later works. But the most significant texts of *Swords like Lips* are still bitter poems, impregnated with the despair we diagnosed in the earlier work.

In these poems of immersion into the abyss, intuition will express what the deep feeling of the soul is like; how it feels and how man feels. Let us examine the poem entitled «At the Bottom of the Well,» to which later was added the subtitle «The Buried Man» in order to clarify the substance and the sense of the poem. This is a song to death intuited in its concrete reality; not death in the abstract, but with reference to the flesh and the blood of the poet himself. It is the favorite theme of the romantic poets, and Enrique Gil greated it with notable delicacy; from him to Aleixandre there is a great change, and by studying this change one can see the extraordinary transformation of the romantic sensibility and of the romantic way of being that has occurred during the past one hundred years. Earlier in Spanish poetry they did not reach this serenity in horror or this impassive fixation on the macabre:

> *There at the bottom of the well where the little flowers,*
> *where the lovely daisies do not wave,*
> *where there is no wind or perfume of man,*
> *where the sea never imposes its threat,*
> *there, there that silence is quiet*
> *like a noise choked by a fist.*
> ....

> *A board at the bottom, oh unnumbered well,*
> *that illustrious smoothness that proves*
> *that a back is contact, it is dry cold,*
> *..*
> *Asleep like fabric*
> *I feel the grass grow, the smooth green*
> *that is uselessly waiting to be curved.*

It is a matter of expressing the unusual: the buried man living death as a prolongation of life and the sensations of the cadaver. Death is a reality through which one can stay in contact with life. The person capable of understanding the reality of being and the reality of life like this will feel them affected by death, anticipations of death, and this feeling makes up the personal note of the theme. Notice the radical ambiguity of the intuition and the way the two planes, the two situations life-death, are joined to create a living-in-death of extraordinary resonance.

Having begun the process of clarifying the poetry, we should ask if the transition from *Passion of the Earth* to *Swords like Lips* presupposes a real development. The author and the majority of the critics seem to think so, but I disagree with this majority. Part of the vigor revealed in the prose poems becomes diluted or muffled in the latter poems. On reading *Passion of the Earth,* the sensation of access to a different world is stronger, as is the feeling of immersion into a chaos whose crudeness must be preserved.

Some poems in *Swords like Lips* seem very close to the spirit that informed the earlier work. For example the already cited «At the Bottom of the Well,» where one notices the tension of the strange, no less intense because it is refined, and a kind of impassioned hallucination which was at that time characteristic of Aleixandre's poetry. Since Bousoño in his monograph has already carefully studied the characteristic use of the conjunction *or,* the use of negation and other syntactical devices of Aleixandre, there is no need to dwell on an analysis of these extremes, but I should like to stress the exactitude of Bousoño's conclusions especially with regard to the different values of the conjunction *or* in Aleixandre's poetry and above all in *Swords like Lips.*

Since the variable meaning of the *or* in these poems has been established, it is easy to understand how surprising identifications were created by means of its use. The conjunction is used with a comparative meaning in order to divert the reader's attention from the object named or the reality designated and toward an imaginative level where the object *or* the reality appears transfigured; while they maintain their identity, they are reverberant with meaning and fuller because of their contact with the other images or realities which have been incorporated into the verse through the simple device of the conjunction. With few artifices, Aleixandre manages to suggest relationships existing between different orders of reality and also an equivalency between them. In these poems, everything is joined together; the real and the unreal, associated in the vision, must also mingle in the poem and, for it to be faithful to the creative intuition, the fusion must be as complete and as inextricable as possible.

Critical analysis defines the elements of the composition and determines their source, but after this is done, the poem must be reconsidered in its natural «confusion,» absolutely loving and necessary; because if we eliminate the jumbled nature and the darkness of the poem when we try to explain it, we are destroying the power of the effect attained which shows the natural mingling of light and shadow that makes up the world of the poet.

As I indicated, in *Swords like Lips* the presence of love is reiterated and becomes more insistent. Thus it is, we might say, an anticipation of the way the theme will be treated in the succeeding work. The poem «The Most Beautiful Love» leaves no doubt about Aleixandre's intuition of love: love-passion, love-flame, love-destruction, love-beast. Naturally the expression conserves and communicates in the poetic object the author's original vision:

> But I found myself a shark in the form of affection;
> no, no; in the form of a well loved shark;
> clean squalus, extendible heart, burning or crime,
> delicious possession that consists of the sea.

In a very few lines reflections of a coherent vision are accumulated which should be studied closely. The image of the shark, because of the voracity associated with it, represents the avidity and the possessive anxiety of love; the need to devour, to make the beloved one's own, is sharply stated as is also the ambiguous invention of labeling the shark as «clean,» and resolving in the last line the question raised by the disjunctive at the end of the preceding line. The end can be explained: «burning or crime?» «No, delicious possession that consists of the sea.»

There is perhaps in these lines a reminiscence of Lautre-amont's magnificent fragment in the second canto of *Maldoror*, dedicated to the love between Maldoror and the female shark. There is a great difference between this selection and Aleixandre's poem, but I wonder if the image of the shark does not derive from the brilliant hallucinations of the French poet. The relationship seems clearer in the following lines which almost seem a gloss of Lautreamont's passage:

> *Thus, without ending mutely that bloody coupling,*
> *breathing in above all a thick ink,*
> ....
> *A mouth imposing like a bestial fruit,*
> *like a dagger that threatens love from the sand,*
> *a bite that might take in all the water or night,*
> *a name that resounds like a rolling roar,*
> *everything whispered by lips I adore.*

This chain of images prolongs and completes the former series and rounds it out. The reader, overwhelmed by the imagery, gradually becomes possessed by the poetic vision and pervaded by everything the poem suggests.

Another part of this book introduces one of Aleixandre's great themes: the integration of poet and nature by means of death. One can see a variation in the poem cited above: death will be a rebirth to another life realized in nature; it will be an «ultimate birth» (title of a poem in *Swords like Lips* and of a book published in 1953). Death as a liberation from existential contingency; as a growing to more life and a transmutation of the individual self into the great whole.

The circle closes: death-love-death, with a positive ac-ceptance of death, the inevitable passage to the desired integra-tion into the whole. The poet approaches a pantheistic concep-tion of the world, and the stylistic devices used to express his intuition of the transformation give emphasis to interesting peculiarities. This «Ultimate Birth» takes place lucidly and happily. The repetition of the adjective makes this clear:

> To end, this alert attitude.
> Alert, alert, alert.

In the same way he jubilantly points to the sounds of the dawning day of the birth: «When the day is born a town cry or jubilations are heard,» identifying the voices of dawn with happiness, with canticles of happiness. The metaphors tend to produce a similar impression: «I am tall like youth which doesn't cease,» suggesting images of vitality and force. Through a careful selection of images, Aleixandre brings into the poem the same pervasive vigor of his intuition of individual life ascending to a «definitive birth into the unitary earth.»(6)

The poem «Salon» presents a notable contrast between this magical birth and life as lived at a party. And what a party! The heptasyllabic rhythm and the assonant rhyme of the vowel *a* lend the composition the fast cadence of the gallop and of the voluntary monotony of loud hammering. The turns of a fast repetitive dance which is at the same time a parade of incisive, synthetic allusions:

> A music or nard
> or some spiderwebs,
> a jug of exhaustion
> and of powders or mother-of-pearl. . .

Life presented as a faded party; the valkyries, by use of the characteristic *or*, are turned into «fainting ladies»; the bird is made of «paper»; love does not have the dramatic violence of other poems: «love is algae.» The poet uses various techniques to define the intuitions and to fix the nature of each one: different meter, rhythm and use of adjectives respond to different stimuli. In order to express opposite visions, there is continuous variation of the forms utilized to adapt the intuition, to embody it, to objectify it.

The Intermediate Stage

In 1934 Aleixandre was awarded the National Literature Prize for *Destruction or Love,* published in the following year.

At the homage organized to celebrate his success, I had the opportunity to meet the poet, and what impressed me the most was his open, child-like smile in a calm and confident face.

A hopeful and hasty first reading of this work revealed to me an Aleixandre more master of the means of expression, more sure of himself and of his poetry than in the earlier works. But that intense Aleixandre inflamed with the flash of illumination did not go with the physical man, as I discovered during that long-ago noon in Madrid; it didn't match up with the clear smile and the transparent face that gave no evidence of the dark struggle of elemental forces captured in his poetry. The man Aleixandre was soothing and reserved, and from him emanated calmness and serenity; he was a smiling, self-controlled man.

Destruction or Love, which I had just read, was turbulent and extreme, written apparently by an impassioned soul struggling to clarify itself and the world. But this was still an intermediary stage. The process of poetic clarification begun in *Swords like Lips* (in relation to *Passion of the Earth* and not to *Ambit*) was continued in the new book; indeed, it made an accelerated turn toward the light which anticipated imminent changes in his work. Some parts of these poems could properly be considered in terms of his next stage of poetic creation.

In this regard, *Destruction or Love* is an important book: given the nature of his creation at that time, greater expressive transparency could not be attempted. When the vision changes, the expressive form will change; in various places in this book we find unmistakable anticipations of this transformation.

A significant example is found in the poem «The Light». The very fact that he was inspired by such a theme indicates a change in the nature of his creation and in the stimulus that determines it. The one who must and does sing of the light does so because his heart enjoys it and overflows with it. Expression becomes luminous, and this joyous luminosity, plenitude of life, is expressed in a chain of interrogative images:

> *Where do you come from, where are you from, loving form*
> *which I feel breathe,*
> *Which I feel like a breast that would contain a music,*
> *Which I feel like the sound of celestial harps,*
> *now almost crystalline like the sound of worlds?*
> *Where are you from, celestial tunic with the form*

> *of the luminous ray*
> *who caresses a forehead that lives and suffers,*
> *that loves like the living?*

Light is a living «loving form,» a breast full of harmony, sounds of heavenly music, the whisper of worlds and also a «celestial» tunic. And there follow serene, truly illuminating images which establish an identity in diversity, more important for their effects than for their meaning.

The efficacy of the system is based on the preciseness of the images. If they have a felicitous impact it is because the reader accepts as natural and exact the treatment of light as the world's covering, «celestial tunic,» and also because the reading of the poem releases impressions which refer to common experiences in whose depths the poetic word resounds like the true word, connected with an instant of life, of our own individual life.

Perhaps the most revealing part of the poem is the end: the acknowledgement of light as messenger which completes the vision. Having established the unity of the world through the unity of the essential nature of sounds, lights, atmospheres, feelings, it is insinuated that all of this announces a higher presence. This is a burst of Aleixandrine pantheism which becomes so sharp in *Shadow of Paradise.*

Destruction or Love is, as the title indicates, a book dedicated to singing of love in its living, annihilating flame: love-destruction. Without the roughness of the earlier poems, without recourse to images of cruel violence like that of the shark to express the living reality of love. Love is sweetness, but threatened, the triumph of life and the eventual destruction of life. Love, exposed, always threatening. The very nature of love is to endanger the balance of that which exists; to rupture the established and to overpower all that surrounds it.

Pedro Salinas, who reviewed this work, points out how «the romantic vision of the essential identification of love and death is corroborated in various passages of the book; sometimes tragically. . . at other times languidly and in a muffled way.»(7) The impulse follows this double course: sometimes it is stated in despairing tones and other times it seems almost faint. A notable example of the first aspect is the ending of the poem «Come Always, Come»:

> *Come, come, death, love; come quickly, I destroy you;*
> *come, for I want to kill or to love or to die or*
> > *to give you everything;*
> *come, for you roll like a fickle stone,*
> *confused like a moon that asks me for my rays!*

«They Loved Each Other» is an example of the tendency to state with melancholy the fatality of love that leads to death. To express this, Aleixandre does not need to rely on technical complexity or verbal extremes, he needs only to refer to the past, situating the vision in a distance. Sweet love «was,» and when he speaks of it, instead of making it present, he recollects it as past, suggesting its inevitable frustration or the total realization of love as necessary for death.

There is a coherence of Aleixandre's vision and feeling of the world since, when one feels death as a continuation of life, as life in another sphere assimilated into the natural, it is logical that one will see the plenitude of love in death and destruction as a means of transformation of the two. The annihilation of the world and of the balance of nature may be a necessary condition for the plenitude of love.

The romantic double vision of the identification of love-death mentioned by Salinas is not the only vision of love expressed in this work. Together with love-destruction, we find love-plenitude, a love achieved through coincidence and harmony, but even here the confusion of two souls alludes in some way to a new life very similar to death.

If all great poetry revolves around love-death, the center of man's life and being, Aleixandre's poetry seldom strays from this theme except on those occasions when he delights in creating a new image which has stuck in his imaginagion, as in «Cobra.» It is not strange, then, given the importance of the theme, that the poetic substance of his early works should be treated in his later ones in new forms and through more refined intuitions.

This reiteration of the theme allows us to follow the direction of his work as it develops. In connection with a motif studied above, I shall examine the «Song to a Dead Girl.» Here he returns to the perception of the body, buried but still living, which he had treated in *Swords like Lips*. The differences, however, are great. The first and most obvious is that now the person who is buried is a girl, and the elegiac tone has a slight erotic tinge that reveals the feeling of the poet with extreme delicacy. From the formal point of view, the images that express the charm of the dead girl are very beautiful.

The impression produced by «At the Bottom of the Well» was necessarily sad and bitter; this «Song,» while sad, is not bitter. The dead girl does not decay: she is water and fresh shore:

> *I want to know why you are now water,*
> *those fresh banks where naked feet bathe in foam.*

To indicate the other life, he uses an isolated touch here and there: «your loose hair» caressed by the sun, and especially in the expressiveness of the following lines which communicate nostalgia and frustration in the words themselves and in their conception:

> *Tell me why your heart like a tiny jungle*
> *waits under the earth for impossible birds,*

The economy of these lines is so fine that one could almost say the next two were unnecessary. In them, he clarifies the image by identifying the «impossible birds» with the song of dreams. But this clarification prolongs the poem and illuminates the sense of the organizing intuition which depicts the buried girl spying on life, listening to the pulse of nature (and perhaps participating in it), aware of the beauty of the world, with an expectation doomed to permanent frustration.

The girl and the buried man are neighbors in death, close in the after-life they dream. What varies between the two poems is not the awareness or the conception of the other-world of death, but the expression, which has become more luminous and richer in suggestive possibilities. This reiteration and renovation of the theme with little change in substance demonstrates the unity of Aleixandre's work during this first period which closes with *Destruction or Love.*

Plenitude of the Poet

In 1944 after the parenthesis of the Civil War and almost ten years after the publication of the last volume, the most seasoned, compact and luminous of his books, *Shadow of Paradise,* was published. When it appeared, it caused a great commotion among young Spanish and Spanish American poets, who immediately began to «aleixandrize» with a frenzy. For some time the majority of these poets recognized Aleixandre as their master, and he, from his house in Metropolitan Park in Madrid, maintained a correspondence with many of them. This excess of imitators and popularizers did not tarnish the brilliance of Aleixandre's work nor did the poems of *Shadow of Paradise* loose any of the early quality.

This is a unified book, solidly worked, and although the earlier ones also were in the sense that they were not mere collections of poems but rather whole works organized around two or three major themes, in this work the coherence and the system are more complete in that unity of substance and unity of theme are merged. The poems present different facets and aspects of one single vision: the vision of paradise recollected in the nostalgia of its irremediable loss.

Nostalgia is a state of mind which embellishes what is evoked. The poems of *Shadow of Paradise* sparkle because the poetic objects in themselves are radiant, luminous, and as hard as precious stones. The poet sings the images of his vision as well as their setting, their place in a natural landscape which is beautiful, not because it is idealized, but because its spell depends on a precision of detail which communicates to the reader in all of its rich and prickly pullulation the spectacle discovered by the poet's imagination.

The poetic vision is complete, extensive, inclusive and detailed; the visionary landscape is at the same time natural and beautiful. The sharpness of the vision produces the natural effect of placing character and figures in their true perspective and with their proper form. Everything stands out in relief and in proportion within a sustained lyrical current that flows with unchanging rhythm, fertile and secure in itself and in the springs which nourish it. The plasticity of the poetic object forged in exact and clearly resolved forms stands out in the luminous atmosphere of the book, and this light is appropriate to the expression of the reality addressed.

Paradise: triumph of light, world woven of light requires this transpatent diction, this clarity and terseness of word in accord with the unfolding vision of the book. But the expressive clarity, the simple word and its derivative transparency might be deceptive; the feeling is deep, and to get to it, the reader must seek out the various levels of meaning in which the creative imagination moves.

The way to the light was traced in Aleixandre's previous work, and one could presuppose how his poetry was going to evolve but not the rapidity of the change. Apart from internal reasons which depend on the distinct quality of the vision presented in this book, another probable influence toward change is the new generation of 1936 which, with books like *El rayo que no cesa* by Miguel Hernández and *Abril* by Luis Rosales, declares from the very beginning a preference for expressive clarity. It would be interesting to study the influence of these younger poets on the generation of 1925, but here I merely mention it as one of the causes contributing to the change we have noted in Aleixandre's attitude.

Shadow of Paradise does not represent a rupture with what preceded it; it attempts to be and is a culmination. When I studied the poetry of Gerardo Diego, I showed how there is a double or triple current in his creation which permits him to exploit alternately and at times simultaneously an innovative vein and a traditional vein. We do not find this dualism in Aleixandre: his evolution is linear, beginning with the simple, relatively unproblematical world of *Ambit,* followed by the plunge into the abyss in *Passion of the Earth,* living in the convulsive world of *Swords like Lips,* and then through the agonizing *Destruction or Love* and the desolate *World Alone,* to arrive at the clarity of *Shadow of Paradise* which is sustained in *History of the Heart.* An itinerary without enigma: every now and then devices and techniques from an earlier stage reappear, but normally they are adapted to the current intuitions.

The coherence of *Shadow of Paradise* makes one think of an ongoing vision, almost a vision with a plot. The figures of this radiant ambience have an animated existence and as a whole they make up a harmonious and moving plot that attracts and wins over the reader.

Dámaso Alonso, in his study of the world revealed in this book, classifies it as auroral, and he stresses one bit of information helpful to an understanding of Aleixandre's creative attitudes: the «City of Paradise,» one of the poems, is Málaga, and its river is the river of the author's childhood: «it is the blue childhood of the poet himself elevated to an Andalusian paradise.»(8) He goes on: «Weariness of the world leads the eyes back to the world's childhood; weariness of man makes him look back toward his remote childhood as toward a distant paradise.»

With regard to the first statement, suffice it to say that when a selection of paradisiacal poems was published in Málaga in 1952, Aleixandre acknowledged the influence of his native city and countryside on them. There is no doubt that the radiant hallucinatory vision of *Shadow of Paradise* derives from a reality, and since it is the reality of childhood which seems a paradise lost to the eyes of the adult, this provided the precipitant of the book. This is the opinion of Dámaso Alonso, and his interpretation of this matter as well as his general thesis seem incontravertible.

The principle theme of *Shadow of Paradise* is a dawning or, more specifically, the dawn. The poet says: «Canticle of the light from awareness of paradise.»(9) The image of the buried man is exchanged for the less truculent but no less romantic image of the person in exile. Uninhabited dawn reduced to elemental forces, but seen and lived by man, who is recreated in its beauty and delights in all that is revealed and sparkles in it. As I have said, the development of the book, or of the series of poems which comprise the volume is harmonious (although it might seem exaggerated to insist on their unitary nature to the point of considering the different compositions as fragments of one broader piece which gives them full meaning); it expresses the initial radiant beauty, its transformation by the eye of man, and his sudden awareness of his destiny.

Not only is this Aleixandre's most ambitious book, it is also the most sustained in its successes; it seem as if this intuition was gradually gaining clarity and profundity as the poet expressed it in the word. In his work, Aleixandre attempted to take in the cosmos and since, fortunately, his mind is lyrical and not philosophical, he had to give himself over to the transcription and transfiguration of his visions. This is what he did in his earlier books, but *Shadow of Paradise* forced him to greater and more effective precision because of the need for clarity imposed on him by the theme.

Continuations

Between *Shadow of Paradise* and *History of the Heart*, Aleixandre published two other books: *World Alone* in 1950, and *Ultimate Birth* in 1953. The first named was published late but written between 1934 and 1936 and, in the opinion of the poet, «its style marks the transition between *Destruction or Love* and *Shadow of Paradise.*»(10) In reality it is a prolongation of the earlier style with reference to a different kind of preoccupation. The vision reaches a point of maximum desolation, of intense pessimism: the world is empty, «man does not exist» (the title of the poem which sums up this visionary impression). Paradoxically, love, delirious love, does exist in the best tradition of Aleixandrine romanticism:

I don't know what death is, if one kisses the mouth.
I don't know what it is to die. I don't die. I sing.
I sing dead and decayed like a brilliant bone,
radiant before the moon like purest crystal.

I want to strees these lines from «Torment of Love» because, having slipped from the soul, these laments may seem dissonant when compared with other poems in the book (if not in their tone, in their accent). They serve to corroborate the impression that, always and under all circumstances, Vicente Aleixandre feels the need to write of love, of living love, in his poetry.

Ultimate Birth is the least unitary of the later works. It is comprised of three series of poems grouped according to theme or inspiration; there are also several unrelated poems.

As we saw when we commented one poem in *Swords like Lips,* «ultimate birth» means dying. The first part of the book is made up of thirteen poems which repeat the emotion of death and the intuition of this afterlife as previously treated in diverse forms. Examples of the titles in this section are: «The Buried Man,» «The Buried Lovers,» «The Dead Man.» This series serves as an overview of Aleixandre's preoccuppations concerning this theme.

In a different section, there are five paradisiacal poems written in the same mood and spirit as the poems in *Shadow of Paradise*. Nine «portraits and dedications» are statements of admiration and homage to friends and poets. The poems of circumstance are general in nature.

These two books represent moments when Aleixandre's artistic creation followed from stimuli expressed better in earlier poems; they respond to sporadic enthusiasm without the spirit and tension achieved in his major works. With the exception of a few isolated poems, we do not find his best poetry in these works.

Contemplation of Paradise

The explicit confession was unnecessary, but we have it; the supporting clarification was not necessary either, but Aleixandre's acceptance speech given before the Royal Academy on January 22, 1949 provides them. I shall transcribe here some lines from «In the Life of the Poet: Love and Poetry»:

> *What does the person in love feel? At the peak of life, in the vitalized eccstasy of love, what is harbored in the heart of man? 'The desire of death is felt' as a poet, a person has presumed. Death here is not death, it is the supreme word of love: it is immortality.*(11)

Love, plenitude of life, overwhelming the heart of man and making him desire death in order to perpetuate the instant of plenitude, in order to make the possession irrevocable.

If *Passion of the Earth* describes the descent of the poet into hell, *History of the Heart* suggests his metaphoric ascent into «heaven.» Behind the word and the image, one senses a sound, an imprecise fragrance; one senses the closeness of an invisible continent from which emanate partially undeciphered and perhaps indecipherable signals whose origin we can divine when we notice the aura that surrounds them. In this book, Aleixandre has sought «to tell pure emotion,» as Machado said, instead of more or less suggestive anecdotes. Consequently, the texture

of the poems is woven with the thread of emotions and, although
the motifs are different, the result is harmonious; the differences
and the shadows are resolved in a higher instance, in intuition,
alive and crystallized in the word, they propose our delight.

Heaven and hell are within man; he finds them in himself.
The impulse toward the heights is as natural as the impulsion
to sound the depths; we seek to know ourselves integrally and
we think that the key might lie in these zones, hidden by the
dazzle of light or darkness. (Aleixandre found poetry in between
bedazzlement and darkness). And why hell first? Antonio
Machado replies: «When the poet has explored all of his hell he,
like Dante, will come back 'to reexamine the stars'; he will
discover, eternal discoverer of Mediterraneans, the marvel of
things and the miracle of reason.»(12)

I have said above that Aleixandre is, above all, a poet of
love. But never so much as in *History of the Heart*, whose title
captures exactly the tone of the whole work (and could be extended
to his whole production). A lyrical, confidential, sometimes
secret tone. Aleixandre sought to express the discoveries of the
heart; he sought to «communicate,» as he says, what was deepest
and most himself in order to enter into the reader and make him
his own by surrendering himself to him.(13)

Let us pause to clarify the meaning of «communicate,»
since I disagree with Aleixandre. I believe that poetry is not
communication nor, insofar as it is poetry, does it seek this effect.
To communicate, prose is quite sufficient. Poetry is the expression of an intuition, not the transmission of a mood which in itself
matters little to the reader. A young critic, Jaime Gil de Biedma
(and before him another young critic Carlos Barral) states: «an
initial reservation: in many cases, the one who affirms that poetry is communication only means to state that poetry fulfills a com-
municative function; this seems to me the case of Vicente Aleixandre: poetry is, *for him,* communication. Aleixandre speaks as a
poet and a reader and what he says is a personal truth, not a
critical truth.»(14)

If Aleixandre uses the verb «communicate» in the sense of
«say» then it is an acceptable expression: but if «communicate»
means the transmission of experience then the term, in relation to
lyrical poetry, ought to be rejected, since poetry is not the sum of
living but the expression of intuitions suggested by it. The poem
is a certain kind of reality, an object created with words, and its

value depends on the quality of expression independent of the intensity and sincerity of the experience.

We mean, then, that Aleixandre's work is a confession required by his desire, by his need to reach and strike the recipient of the poem. But this characteristic is not sufficient to achieve the stated purpose. In *History of the Heart* confidentiality is more direct but if it impresses that is because the poem, the object created by a departure from living, is capable of arousing certain impressions which are aesthetic in nature. There is a clear play of equivalences between living-word-living, and intuition serves as the mechanism for apprehending and transforming.

In this work by Aleixandre, this play is successful. His poetic diction is appropriate to the amorous theme. The verse is like a slow-moving river which permits an insistent search for the shading, for the fluidity and the abundance of precise images, questions, surprises. . .

History of the Heart, like all of Aleixandre's books, is full of elemental movement, but unlike the other works, here vision is replaced by recollection: imagination yields to memory although the remembering may be imaginative and with a tendency to feed on its own energy, the way that poems of his earlier periods derived from imagination and were nourished by memory. And since memories, or at least certain memories, coincide more readily with the memories of others than does imagination, this work (as the author himself says in the introduction to *My Best Poems*)(15) is the one which «has resonated in the most various, scattered, different and even contrary hearts.» This does not surprise me since I vividly recall the first time I read it and I know how forcefully the poet's penetration of the magical world of love impresses. And I wonder why he did not include among his «best poems» the one titled «The Dream» which, because of the cruel and delicate lucidity of the intuition, is very similar to the poems of Charles Baudelaire and even to certain pages from Rainer Marie Rilke, at the same time that it is genuinely Aleixandrine:

> *There are moments of solitude*
> *when the heart, realizes, astounded, that it does not love.*
> *We have just raised up, tired: the day dark.*
> *Someone is sleeping, innocent, still on that bed.*
> *But perhaps we sleep. . . Ah, no? we move.*

And we are sad, quiet.   The rain, out there, insists.
Morning of slow fog, impious.   How alone we are!
....
And the only sound is the paused breathing of someone,
of the one who, over there, serene, beautiful is sleeping
and dreaming that you do not love her, and you are her
dream.

The poem's economy couldn't be simpler.   Analysis reveals
it to be made up of some concrete, even prosaic, notations
preceded by the initial statement which emerges from the sudden
awareness of a reality: non-love.   To endow this statement
with the shocking character which will make it dazzling, the poet
chooses a fortunate device: the sudden awareness coincides
with awakening, it is an awakening.   Immediately he records
another fact: «the day dark.»   The knowledge of «non-love»
is fraught with shadows and these shadows and the sleep of the
person who sleeps in them make us wonder if «non-love» may not
also be a dream.

This poem does not attempt to solve a problem but, as I
suggested above, to express an intuition in which there are
doubts and twists, like the one insinuated in the suspicion of
the dream, because of the possibility of living an improbable
dream.   The external events, rain, mist, solitude, clarify the
mood as they describe the ambience in that the mood is influenced
and formed by the external.   In the lines omitted, there is a brief
description of activities.   The man looks outside and finds it sad,
inhospitable.   Silence, broken only by the breathing of the
«beautiful» sleeping woman in whose dream the poet discovers
the confirmation of his thought.

This analysis serves as an example of what could be done with
any other poem.   This poem does give us an idea of the climate of
the work even though, as I have stressed, it is a poem of non-love
instead of love.   In every instance, the selection of the material
was careful and intentional, and I would not exclude the possibility that beneath the intention and the care, there filtered in
through the imagination of the poet elements from other sources.
Not what we would call «influences,» but elements deriving from
the unconscious assimilation of other worlds which harmonize with
the poet's intuition.   It is well known that the work of art,
painting, poem, sculpture or sonata, is a legitimate and effective

experience.

The agreement between the attitude and the mode of feeling explains why I commented on the similarity with parts of Baudelaire and Rilke. Aleixandre's poetry approaches theirs in its sense of melancholy and secretness which produces the images. The poem holds unexpected discoveries, as the clarity of the language belies the element of surprise and revelation.

In some of the poems in this book, Aleixandre captures the feeling of love with beauty and clear outlines. He found in his heart something worthy of being said and expressed it in proper form with precise and suggestive imagery, with clean and simple word. There are pages in *History of the Heart* where the poetry, inspiring and pulsing, flows from the heart of the poet to the heart of the reader.

NOTES

1. «Confidencia literaria» in *Entregas de poesía,* reprinted in *Obras completas,* 1968, p. 1440.

2. *La poesía de Vicente Aleixandre* (Madrid: Insula, 1950).

3. Because of their length, the prose poems from *Passion of the Earth* have not been translated in their entirety.   «Death or the Waiting Room» appears in *Obras completas,* 1968, pp. 181-183.

4. «Clothing and serpent» appears in *Obras completas,* 1968, pp. 195-196.

5. «The World Is Well Made» appears in *Obras completas,* 1968, pp. 233-234.

6. «Note to the first edition,» *Ultimate Birth,* in *Obras completas,* 1968, p. 602.

7. *Literatura española del siglo XX.* 2nd ed. (México: Antigua Librería Robledo, 1949), p. 213.

8. *Poetas españoles contemporáneos* (Madrid: Editorial Gredos, 1952), p. 309.

9. The citation reads: «Cántico de la luz desde la conciencia del paraíso»; I find only the following statements by the poet: «cántico de la luz desde la conciencia de la oscuridad» in «Notas previas» reprinted in *Obras completas,* 1969, p. 1472, and «es un canto a la luz desde la conciencia de la oscuridad» in

«Nota sobre *Sombra del paraíso* para unos estudiantes ingleses» in *Obras completas,* 1968, p. 1478.   These two citations suggest that the translation should read «canticle of the light from awareness of the darkness» instead of «paradise.»

10.   «Nota previa a *Mundo a solas*» in *Obras completas*, 1968, p. 1471.

11.   Cited in *Obras completas*, 1968, p. 1322.

12.   *Los complementarios* (Buenos Aires: Editorial Losada, 1957), P. 119.

13.   Poesía, comunicación» in *Obras completas,* 1968, pp. 1581-1583.

14.   «Prólogo a T. S. Eliot: *Función de la poesía y función de la crítica*» (Barcelona: Biblioteca Breve, n. d.), p. 16.

15.   «A 'Poemas paradisíacos'» in *Obras completas,* 1968, pp. 1453-1455.

THE ISAKOWER PHENOMENON AND THE DREAM SCREEN

Kessel Schwartz
University of Miami

Much of the early poetry of Vicente Aleixandre reveals his view of nature and the world through subjective connotations which relate to a number of conflicts, anxieties, and unconscious fantasies. The poet clarifies some of this poetry, rooted in his unconscious depths, by combining creative and destructive impulses in the apparently ambivalent equation that love equals death. In spite of juxtaposing these and other dissimilarities, Aleixandre, through his very disorientation, which simulates the psychic processes themselves, and by indulging in a kind of free association, transmutes into artistic and understandable form a variety of thinly disguised wishes.

The sea, probably the most prevalent symbol of his poetry, stresses one important aspect of that subconscious process. Undoubtedly, during Aleixandre's youth, Málaga impressed the sea on his consciousness. Water (along with the sea and ocean) in dreams has the symbolic meaning of mother, and, in association with youthful innocence, happiness, and the breast, it is constantly used with this meaning in Aleixandre's poetry. Unconscious forces rather than surrealistic experimentation account for the recurring breast motif and accompanying fantasies. Indeed, Aleixandre himself rejects the label of surrealist.(1) In this subconscious recall Aleixandre constantly juxtaposes the sea with the beach, moon, teeth, tongue, throat, and breast. In many of his poems he seems to use the sea as a surface on which to project his images in a manner analogous to the «dream screen. »

According to Isakower, a person falling asleep who sees dark masses approach and is unable to ascertain the division between his body and the masses, reproduces a little baby's sensations of falling asleep at the breast. This phenomenon is also associated with well-known hypnagogic manifestation of an auditory and

tactile nature, involving mouth sensations and especially bodiless-
ness, floating, and sinking. The drowser feels small in the
presence of something large or heavy and may vaguely perceive
something indefinite or shadowy and of vast size.(2)   Bertram
D. Lewin, complementing this concept, postulates a dream
screen as «the surface on to which a dream appears to be projected.   It is the blank background, present in the dream, though
not necessarily seen, and the visually perceived action in ordinary
manifest dream content takes place on it or before it.»(3)   The
representation of the mother's breast during nursing (the dream
screen) may involve various solid or convex shapes or fluid objects
which serve as screen equivalents and the imaginary fulfillment
of a wish to sleep and a breast to sleep at.   Later events and
situations are projected onto the original blankness (an image of
the breast during the infant's sleep) as if it were a cinematic
screen.   In other words the «dream screen has the metapsycho-
logical structure of a dream, forming the background or projection
drop for the dream picture.»(4)

These phenomena are often accompanied by loss of ego
boundaries, visions of white clouds, receding waves, vaporous
mists, roses or pinkish color (the aureole of the breast), white and
blue contrasts (the breast and the veins), and the constant implica-
tion of thirst related at the same time to concepts of dry, sandy
desert wastes.   A casual examination of Aleixandre's poetry
reveals the presence of the above elements to an intrusive degree.
In *Ambit,* his earliest collection, these symbols of blue and white
interspersed with the idea of dust, mouth and dream, limitless
forms, and especially the moon (a standard mother symbol of
regeneration), which through its curved surface is homologous to
a dream screen, are constant.   The breast symbolism, mouth
sensation, and ecstatic states often seem to relate to the withdrawn
aspects and dry-thirst-tongue and mouth sensations.

More clearly, in the extra-rational *Passion of the Earth*
Aleixandre combines his need for loving and being loved with
breast fantasies in the prose poems «Love Is not Relief,» «Death
or the Waiting Room,» and «Being of Hope and Rain,» which
contains symbols of breast, teeth, new born child, lips, dryness,
tongue, and food bag, together with a floating curtain like a sheet
of rain and a concave mirror.   «Life» shows us a moon-colored
mermaid, her breast like a mouth: «she took out her wounded
breast, split in two like a mouth, and she tried to kiss me on the

dead shadow. . . She didn't have another breast.» The poet rejects his death, related to that of the mermaid who gasps for breath on the surface of the sea. The idea of eating and being eaten by an object is also a way of becoming united with it; in this case, the presence of the mermaid, representative of the primal mother,(5) is significant.

In «Yearning for the Day» the poet, on the surface of a bubble, cannot find «the flesh destined for him.» Lost on the ocean against the background of a wave composed of a handful of umbrellas, he wets his tongue in «the sub-sky, the ecstatic blue.» As he fuses with the ocean he views the potential threat of «the throats of the wet sirens,» and, merging with the larger whole, finds «my hand is a shore. My leg another.» The most striking aspect of what Isakower observed involves the blurring of the distinction between different regions of the body, between what is internal and external, and the amorphous character of the impressions conveyed by the sense organs. «Part of the perceptual apparatus observes the body ego as its boundaries become blurred and fused with the external world, and perceptions become localized as sensations in a particular body region.»(6) Aleixandre misses a finger of his hand and is threatened by an earless monster who carries «instead of his word a short scissor, just right for cutting the open explanation. . .» The defenseless poet delivers himself up to the powerful, threatening shears, possibly the manifest element of a dream which frightens the child (a typical awakener is the father's phallus), a true disturber which relates to repressed impulses which may break through as projections.(7) Intruding preconscious or unconscious wishes that threaten to wake the sleeper form visual content and project the sleeper's ego onto the screen. The representation of the body or its parts in the visual content of the dream means that the part is awake and an intruder and disturber of sleep and pure fulfillment. In this poem, the poet indulges in a kind of autocannibalism: «I weep the whole head. It rolls through my breast and I laugh with my fingernails, with the two feet that are fanning me. . .» Sinking and smothering sensations, or the loss of consciousness, are also found in fantasies of oral incorporation. A baby treats the breast as it does its own fingers, which it stuffs into its mouth, indulging in the identical autocannibalism of this poem. This type of anxiety is related to childhood fantasies about the prenatal state, an aspect of which is the child's imagining it

entered into the mother by being swallowed.(8)   Paradoxically,
sleep which brings pleasure also involves the anxiety of being
eaten and dying.   The young baby projects its self-agression onto
the breast, which it then fears as destructive.   The poet is both
buoyed up and supported by the waves and yet is threatened,
a typical reaction of anxiety dreams about merging with a larger
whole and perishing as an individual.

In «Soul under Water» the image of sinking and yet being
supported by the immense sea continues: «If waves ascend, if
you are soaked with all the sad melancholies that were flying
avoiding your touch with their fine hollow wood, they will stop
right in the throat, decapitating you with light, leaving your head
like the flower. . .»(9)   The room in which he finds himself moves
on the fearful waves, and the poet is borne up: «An enormous
extended sea holds me in the palm of its hand asks me for
respect.»   The wish to sleep seems opposed by other wishes
which have escaped the ego's censorship and become conscious,
a symbolism reaffirmed by «Love Suffered,» the last poem of this
collection.

In *Destruction or Love*, «The Jungle and the Sea» shows us
the human ego overwhelmed by elemental forces, repeating the
anxious transmutation of the original pleasure of falling asleep,
not only the active eating process, but (through the fierce animal
attacks with swords and teeth) the passive idea of being eaten, also
a part of the nursing situation.(10)   The fierce attacks and his
need to punish the rejecting virgin forest, «love or punishment
against the sterile trunks,» seem to involve a fear of a father and,
in the fusion through primitive life with animals, may be a kind of
rationalization of the wish (being eaten) «to get back again into the
mother's animal womb.»(11)   Similar themes occur in «After
Death,» complete with threatening tongues, a furious foam, and
a sea which «robs breasts»; «Symphonic Night,» with tongue,
«sweet taste,» and «breasts. . . harpshaped»; and «Total Love,»
with a sea fusion, young teeth, feeding, and breast imagery.

The breast symbolism of «Sea on Earth» again suggests the
dream screen.   Aleixandre seems to use the sea as a surface on
which to project his images:

> *The resonant sea turned into a lance*
> *lies on the dryness like a fish that's drowning,*
> *it clamors for that water that can be the kiss,*

that can be a breast to be torn and inundated.

But the dry moon doesn't respond to the reflection
of the dry scales.

....

Then joy, the dark joy of dying,
of comprehending that the world is a grain that will
come apart,
the one that was born for a divine water,
for that immense sea that lies over the dust.

Joy will consist of coming apart like the miniscule,
of turning into the severe fishbone,
remains of an ocean that like the light went away,
drop of sand that was a giant breast
and that having left the throat like weeping lies here.

Aleixandre's pseudo-animistic theory holds that man returns in death to the place from which he came, to the sea which gave him birth. The state of sleep bears a marked resemblance to the prenatal state, an intrauterine regression which explains the dark joy of fusing with the sea, of returning to the womb. The «giant breast» gives the theoretical genetic origin of the screen, that is, the way it would look to a baby. Aleixandre's fantasy, in contrast to that of adult dreams in which the screen-ocean itself occupies part of the manifest content, is projected on the sea screen in many different forms at the same time. The gigantic breast which comes out of the poet's throat may be viewed as a withdrawal from the breast. It seems gigantic to the tiny observer, for the adult sees the hallucinated mass of extraordinary magnitude as a baby would view it. The dry, frustrating breast explains the «dry» ocean. A desert (camels are called ships of the desert) is a kind of dry ocean, and a dry moon, equally, symbolizes a dry breast. Strikingly, the dream screen frequently represents something inedible, «tasteless or even disagreeable to the mouth such as a. . . desert, or other wastes and barren tracts.»(12) Throughout this poem Aleixandre stresses the relationship of the sea and dryness, as the dry moon fails to respond, and the immense sea lies on the dust. The dryness and sand typify thirst sensations, much as a gritty mouth would be projected onto the breast symbol.

Shadow of Paradise returns to an innocent world of infancy, to a Paradise beyond original sin and knowledge. One aspect of the invisible and formless but directly apprehended breast involves nebulous and ill-defined perceptions, ineffable experiences, and memories of a lost Paradise of contentment which compel a nostalgic return and attraction to infancy. Having only a momentary recall of Paradise, whose substance he has lost, the poet nonetheless evokes the sea and moon, a cosmic fusion of self with the material of the world, and the hidden beauty at the fount of life where naked creatures drank. The poet submerges himself in the womb of mother earth, in his Paradise where «The tongues of innocence/ did not say words» and which is replete with breasts, «breasts of water,» «white teeth,» and the sea, moon, tongues, and throats. Man's tragedy is that to be born is to be cast out of Paradise, the mother's body where everything is given. As Otto Rank stresses, «the rest of life is taken up with efforts to replace this lost Paradise.»(13)

In «It Is Not Enough,» the final poem of the volume and a summation of the metaphysical content of Aleixandre's trip to Paradise and fusion with the earth, we see a cloud through which purple lightning flashes and in which eyes shine with infinite sadness. The cloud appears and then withdraws, dense, dark, and closed, toward the far-off horizon. The poet feels deprived and miserable and exclaims:

Oh mother, mother, only in your arms I feel
my misery! Only on your breast martyrized by my weeping
I surrender my form, only in you I vanish.

Born of the sea and opressed by his own bodily limits, he needs needs his mother's warmth, support, and beautiful breast:

The promise of God, the imagined loving forehead.
How good from you, from your warm earthy flesh,
to watch the pure waves of the beneficent divinity!

The poem fills many of the requisites for the dream screen. The sea appears as waves intangible to his hands. A weighty cloud stops above the water and then withdraws to a vanishing point on the horizon. The poet associates the cloud's withdrawal with a lost happiness, which he specifically connects with his mother and his mother's empty breast:

> *my mother, of warm darkness,*
> *breast alone where the void reigns,*
> *my love, my love, already you, you alone.*

This kind of pure and holy joy, the ecstasy of an infant at his mother's breast, occurs before the child has learned to speak and is thus almost inexpressible, a «happiness without limits.» The poet rocked in «a swaying of sea, of whole stellar sea. . . ,» associates his mother's breast with the promise of God. The horizon and the clouds floating away in a perspective leading to a vanishing point may well symbolize the withdrawn breast. The poet relates his ensuing emptiness to a lack of God, «I felt on my flesh an emptiness of God.» As Dr. Lewin points out:

> The optical impressions produced by the nursing situation attain some permanence in the form of the dream screen, and later in development become associated with and attached on the representatives of concrete ideas. We are then naturally curious to know whether the nebulous and the intense but ill-defined perceptions enter into such unions too. . . The invisible and formless elements become related to invisible and formless things, which are then perceived in the same direct immanent fashion. The invisible in the breast situation may be brought into juncture with God, the invisible, so that he may be perceived in the same way, directly.(14)

Aleixandre suffers a loss of identity or Ego in the absence of God and the breast, «. . . what absence of God on my fallen head / was keeping limitless vigil over my convulsed body?» He tells his mother that only in her bosom «I surrender my form, only in you I vanish.» the poet's use of «deshacer,» to vanish or be consumed, in connection with his mother's breast, recalls unhappy memories related to pleasurable ones in the primitive wish to sleep and to join the mother, to be one with her at the breast and in sleep, to lose individual consciousness or ego and thus, in a sense, to die.

Aleixandre's symbols often appear incomprehensible to the reader, whose sensibilities, nonetheless, quicken to empathize with those of the poet, inspired by the same enigmas which beset us all, as he seeks to recapture an unconscious knowledge and create a unity of perception.

NOTES

1. Vicente Aleixandre, *Mis mejores poemas* (Madrid, 1956) p. 10 and Fernando Charry Lara, *La poesía neorromántica de Vicente Aleixandre* (Bogotá, 1946), p. 31.

2. Otto Isakower, «A Contribution to the Patho-Psychology of Phenomena Associated with Falling Asleep,» *International Journal of Psycho-Analysis,* XIX (1938), pp. 331-345.

3. Bertram D. Lewin, «Sleep, the Mouth, and the Dream Screen,» *The Psychoanalytic Quarterly,* 15 (1946), p. 420.

4. Bertram D. Lewin, «Reconsiderations of the Dream Screen,» *The Psychoanalytic Quarterly,* 22 (1953). pp. 174-99.

5. Otto Rank, *The Trauma of Birth* (New York, 1952), p. 149. See also Geza Roheim, *Gates of the Dream* (New York, 1952), p. 347. Roheim points out that these water beings devour their victims: «. . . the possible interpretation of these man-eating beings as the oral agression in talion form. . .»

6. Isakower, p. 340.

7. See Bertram D. Lewin, *The Psychoanalysis of Elation* (New York, 1950), p. 112; see also Lewin, «Sleep, the Mouth, and the Dream Screen,» pp. 427-433.

8. Lewin, *The Psychoanalysis of Elation,* pp. 107-108.

9. Bertram D. Lewin, «Reconsiderations of the Dream Screen,» p. 187: «. . . the inside of a hollow space or concavity may represent the breast. . .»; see also Sigmund Freud, *The Basic Writings of Sigmund Freud* (New York, 1938), p. 372, in which he claims that boards are women and that «'wood,' generally speaking, seems, in accordance with its linguistic relations, to represent feminine matter.»

10. Lewin, *The Psychoanalysis of Elation,* p. 11.

11. Rank, p. 149.

12. Lewin, «Reconsiderations,» p. 187.

13. Patrick Mullahy, *Oedipus, Myth and Complex* (New York, 1948), p. 163.

14. Lewin, «Reconsiderations,» p. 191.

VICENTE ALEIXANDRE AND HENRI ROUSSEAU:
A COINCIDENCE IN IMAGERY

Gene Steven Forrest
Southern Methodist University

The comparative analysis of literature and the fine arts today is drawing together supporters and critics who are creating a wider acceptance and a greater authority for it. Among these critics is Helmut Hatzfeld who insists on the essentially aesthetic nature of literature and consequently on its close connection with pictorial art.(1) The greatest proof of this phenomenon in our century is the surrealist adventure which, striving to reveal the subconscious image, spontaneously leaps the dividing lines that have traditionally separated the arts in order to launch (among other «amphibian» genres) the «poème-objet» of Bretón and Victor Brauner's «picto-poésie.» Numerous poets of this same period were also distinguished by their drawings which, in some cases, integrally combined the pictorial image with the poetic image: Cocteau, Apollinaire, Alberti, Lorca, Soffici. Based on this reciprocal drawing together of literature and painting, our analysis will develop the clear parallel which exists between the major Spanish surrealist Vicente Aleixandre and one of the most important precursors of surrealist painting, Henri Rousseau.(2)

Where the poet and the French painter coincide is in the suggestive and irrational «image,» a process described by André Bretón in the following terms: «Les poètes, les artistes se rencontrent avec les savants au sein de ces 'champs de force' crées dans l'imagination par le rapprochement de deux images différentes. Cette faculté de rapprochement de deux images leur permet de s'élever au-dessus de la consideration de la vie manifeste de l'objet, . . .Sous leurs yeux, au contraire, cet objet, tout achevé qu'il est, retourne à une suite ininterrompue de latences qui ne lui sont pas particulières et appelent sa transformation.»(3) This transformation of the conventional value of the image corresponds to the «vision» which Carlos Bousoño considers

Aleixandre's major contribution to poetic imagery, which he defines as an «attribution of unreal qualities or functions to an object.»(4)   In a poetic context, this is equivalent to the «réalisme onirisé» attributed to «Le Rêve» (1910), Rousseau's masterpiece, in which a nude woman seated on a red sofa is magically transplanted to an exotic jungle: «C'est le quotidien devenu insolite, et l'exotique familier.»(5)   It is an instantaneous revelation of implausible proportions or contexts which introduce multiple intellectual and emotional suggestions into consciousness.   In other words, the image moves away from having a mainly representational or pictorial value to presenting a mysterious, allusive value; that is, the conventional image becomes abstract by concentrating an evocative, implicit network of meaning around a nucleus of familiar objects.   In accord with its non-representational character, the new image is placed in space without being oriented in time and thus, lacking historical dimension, it becomes an eternal or mythic symbol.   To a great extent, the fascination inspired by myth and the atemporal structure of contemporary literature follows this reciprocal evolution of the visual and the poetic image: «In a non-naturalistic style, . . . the inherent spaciality of the plastic arts is accentuated by the effort to remove all traces of time-value; and since modern art is non-naturalistic, we can say that it is moving in the direction of increased spaciality.   The significance of spacial form in modern literature now becomes clear: it is the exact complement in literature, on the plane of esthetic form, to the developments that have taken place in the plastic arts.»(6)

The image or «vision» which constitutes the coincidence between Aleixandre and Rousseau is the primordial jungle of Eden, populated with fierce wild beasts and serpents, which forms the dynamic center of *Destruction or Love* and *Shadow of Paradise* and is the major theme of the French painter's canvases from 1904 until his death in 1910.   The exotic landscapes of the customs-official Rousseau, just like the aleixandrine evocations of paradise lost, depict clearly delineated objects against an eternal space; flora and fauna are fully illuminated by the light of the sun or of the moon.   And always a magical silence reigns, broken only by the roaring of the beasts or by a bewitching supernatural music.   Let us compare, for example, the delightful composition of flowers and trees filled with a mysterious trilling in the famous «La charmeuse de serpent» (1907) with the following description from «The Poets»:

What a tender accent reigns
in the shadowless woods,
of smooth skins,
the gazelle without name,
a very sweet deer,
lifts its answer
on its forehead for the day!

With linear precision and minimal chromatic complexity (the basic tones predominate; green, balck, white and blue), objects with clear profiles are balanced in a composition whose purity and simplicity are reminiscent of cubism. Another example is the mysterious juxtaposition of the sleeping woman and the beast in the painting «La Bohemienne endormie» (1897) and the following passage from «Goddess» which, without going beyond the objects themselves, beyond the simultaneous realities of woman and beast, suggests a strange feeling of anxiety and innerness:

Asleep across the tiger,
lies her light tress.
Look at her form.   It breathes
across the beautiful skin,
tranquil, majestic.
Who can dare, who alone
would now place his lips
on the joyous light,
almost human, that dreams?
Look at her there!   How alone!
How untouched, touchable?
....
...And a tiger
proudly bears her
like the Hircanian sea,
where she would float spacious,
happy, never offered.

The supremacy of the object and its pure exact representation reveal the deep equivalency of all elements in nature and

an absolute, almost religious attitude toward all that is natural. No matter how irrational the oniric visions of Aleixandre and Rousseau may be, they are always deeply rooted in nature. Just as the single stalk of a plant in a Rousseau landscape receives the same attention and has the same formal importance as the immense sky, in *Destruction or Love* Aleixandre likewise grants equal meaning to a beetle or a snail as to an elephant or the remote sea. This totalizing vision derives from the romantic belief in the superiority of nature over civilization, and therefore Aleixandre and Rousseau in their oniric search for purity and authenticity envision a garden of Eden previous to the appearance of man. Bousoño affirms that *Shadow of Paradise* is just that: «a symphonic vision emanating from and justified by human desire: the desire for purity, for elementalness, for authenticity. . . It is evident, then, that the theme of paradise is a consequence of the central conception of Aleixandre which sees the elemental as the supreme world of existence.»(7) Thus the ingenuousness which gave rise to so many picturesque anecdotes about the life of Rousseau reflects a basically «infantile,» elemental vision, as Tristan Tzara, one of the painter's principle admirers, observes: «Freedom to interpret the world as a Garden of Eden is reserved for those whose childhood has expanded without losing its primordial purity.»(8)

Precisely how is Eden visualized by the Spanish poet and the French painter, and based on what law or philosophy is it formulated? Dámaso Alonso and Carlos Bousoño stress the pantheistic mysticism of Aleixandre in which every element, be it fish, insect or flower, forms a part of the whole, and on joining this whole, on dying, becomes fully realized in what, for Aleixandre, constitutes an «amorous» union: «Because love is an act of de-limitation which shatters our limits and absorbs our ego, it seems for an instant as if one is reincorporated into indivisible nature. Love is, then, destruction, overwhelming annihilation of each one of the lovers who is trying to be the other. . . If love is destruction, then love, anger and hatred are the same from Aleixandre's perspective. They are diverse manifestations of the generic erotic act, the disintegrating force of the principle of individuation.»(9)

In *Destruction or Love*, there are abundant examples of these ambiguous «amorous» or «destructive» encounters: tigers and lions who show their teeth like the beating of a loving heart, the eagle who caresses a rock with his talons, the scorpion and the cobra who only aspire to capture the vital presence. The jungle exoticism of Rousseau's last stage which, up to a certain point, follows the African and Oriental motifs popular among salon painters after Delacroix, goes far beyond a simple decorative or escapist experiment. It is known that for Rousseau there was no divorce between his bourgeois Parisian milieu and the fantastic world of his own creation, and many times the beasts and the serpents in his paintings filled him with such terror that he would run to open the windows of his studio.(10) Like Aleixandre, Rousseau inspires terror in us through the imminent and savage death which peers out from behind each leaf and flower of the jungle, but also like Aleixandre, he surpasses tragedy by focussing on the wider natural context. Thus he presents to us barbarous banquets of tigers, panthers, and birds of prey surrounded by radiant flowers and sky: «If the theme is the law of the jungle, the artist's development is detached and remote. The incident of the struggle is overwhelmed by a luxuriant flora which conpletely dominates the picture. In some of the works Rousseau treats monkeys at play. . . but the effect is strange and sub-humorous. His conception answers the reality of imagination rather than of nature.»(11) This «reality of the imagination,» the juxtaposition of the destructive violence and the bucolic harmony in nature seems to coincide closely with the pantheistic mysticism of Aleixandre. Notice the equivocal posture of beast and victim in «Cheval attaqué par un jaguar» (1910), which rather than a bloody «combat,» suggests a passionate «embrace.» Surrounded by magnificent dense vegetation, the scene seems to indicate fertility and new life instead of destruction and death.

Insofar as a direct influence of Rousseau's work on Aleixandre is concerned, no concrete proof of it exists nor is it essential for our thesis that such proof be ascertained. Even if the poet were unaware of the French painter's work, and this would be highly improbable given his keen interest in painting,(12) that would not affect the clear parallel which links the work of the artist and the poet. Certainly there do exist between the two fundamental differences in temperament, depth, and emphasis (especially the contrast between the smiling surrender of man and his circumstance which caracterizes the work of the naive painter and the deeply pessimistic representation of the «fallen angel» of Aleixander's condemned humanity), but beyond their differences is revealed a unique approach to the oniric, surreal «vision.»

NOTES

1. *Literature through Art: A New Approach to French Literature,* University of North Carolina Studies in the Romance Languages and Literatures, 86 (Chapel Hill: University of North Carolina Press, 1969), p. v.

2. While writing this study, I learned of the excellent unpublished work of Hernán Galilea, «El aspecto onírico en la poesía de Vicente Aleixandre en su relación con el superrealismo en la pintura,» dissertation, Catholic University, 1971; a work which deals with Aleixandre's poetry in light of the surrealist painters Dalí, De Chrico, Magritte, Ernst, etc. with only passing references to Rousseau.   Here I seek to develop these partial allusions more thoroughly.

3. *Le surréalisme et la peinture* (New York: Brentano's, Inc., 1945), p. 130.

4. *La poesía española de Vicente Aleixandre* 2nd. ed. (Madrid: Editorial Gredos, 1956), p. 140.

5. René Passeron, *Histoire de la peinture surréaliste* (Paris: Le Livre de Poche, 1968), p. 81.

6. Joseph Frank, «Spatial Form in Modern Literature,» in *Sewanee Review,* 52, No. 3 (1945), pp. 650-651

7. *La poesía de Vicente Aleixandre,* p. 75.

8. Cited by A. Basler in Jean Bouret, *Henri Rousseau,* Trans. by Martin Leake (Greenwich, Connecticut: New York Graphic Society, 1961), p. 30.

9. *La poesía de Vicente Aleixandre,* pp. 63-64.

10. *Henri Rousseau,* p. 27.   (Bouret)

11. Daniel Catton Rich, *Henri Rousseau* (New York: the Museum of Modern Art, 1946), pp. 60-61.

12. Kessel Schwartz, *Vicente Aleixandre* (New York: Twayne Publishers, Inc., 1970), p. 13.

WORLD ALONE: A COSMOVISION AND METAPHOR OF ABSENT LOVE

Vicente Cabrera
Colorado State University

The poetic work of Vicente Aleixandre from *Passion of the Earth* up to *Shadow of Paradise*,(1) which makes up his first and perhaps richest period,(2) is characterized as much by the unity of the elemental and cosmic conception of its theme as by the coherent and imaginative homogeneity of its diction. This substructure of vision and diction on which the poetry of this period rests is the result of an ongoing evolution in which each book becomes an outgrowth of the former one; that is, a lyrical step forward which, deriving from the earlier work, consolidates a new poetic vision. This evolution, however, is interrupted with the appearance of *Shadow of Paradise,* a work which, although it remans within the cosmic and elemental vision of the others, stylistically represents a change which had not previously occurred, for example, between *Passion of the Earth* and *Swords like Lips,* or between the latter and *Destruction or Love,* the work immediately preceding *Shadow of Paradise.*

There is no doubt that Aleixandre's silence between 1933 and 1944 led critics to suspect some sort of poetic crisis in the writer.(3) But these speculations disappear with the publication of *World Alone* in 1950. Aleixandre says in the introductory note that this book was composed between 1934 and 1936, that is, between *Destruction or Love* and *Shadow of Paradise.* The author also explains that although «chronologically it antecedes it [*Shadow of Paradise*] in composition and therefore in style, in the development of a world to be expressed it is later.»(4) In his note to *My Best Poems,* he adds that *World Alone* is «perhaps the most pessimistic» of his books.(5) This idea has been misinterpreted by critics as they attempt to deal with the whole as a simple negative canto and nothing more. The reason for this pessimism has not been explained nor have the other elements been explored.

These new elements not only enrich the book's cosmovision but also make of this cosmovision a thematic outgrowth of the previously mentioned first period.

Seventeen poems were included in the first edition. Later one was added for the publication of the *Complete Works*, «Final fire,» and three more for the edition which in 1970 Aleixandre stated was the «complete» one: «In a Cemetery,» «Smoke and Earth,» and «Fallen Moon.» In the first poem, «Final Fire,» hope and even the certainty of surviving the final fire of death is found in love:

> *You are as beautiful as the hope of living yet.*
> *As the certainty of loving you day after day.*
> ....
> *Little girl small or sweet who are love or life,*
> *a promise when the fire nears,*
> *a promise of living, of living in May,*
> *without having those flames which are burning the world*
> *reduce you to nothing. . . .*

In the other three, especially in «In a Cemetery» and «Fallen Moon,» the poetic vision is more ambiguous and severe because of the opposition of elements of life and death in the same equation and because of the juxtaposition of doubt and anguish with the drive to survive and integrate himself with the cosmos, expressed in «In a Cemetery» as follows:

> *I still live, yes.   I still live and seek earth,*
> *earth in my arms, while all the air*
> *is filled with its dark birds,*

The poet feels that his cosmic reintegration achieved through death divests it of its negative nature. These four poems do not alter the general spirit of the book; they broaden it by adding new visions which emanate from its matrix: the being and the cosmos in their union and disunion.

The circumstances surrounding this work (the year of its publication, the apparent complications which its style represents in the poetic development of Aleixandre and the late--1970-- inclusion of poems to complete it) have kept it from having the same popularity and impact as the earlier books.(6)   Also the enthusiasm and «stupefaction»(7) produced by *Shadow of Paradise* overshadowed its importance.　But, as will be seen in this study, *World Alone* is intrinsically as artistic as the works published just before and after it.

I

There are three thematic currents in *World Alone:*　love, the cosmos and man.　Although it is impossible to separate one from the other, for the sake of clarity we shall try to study them separately here.

A)　*Love.*　The poet comes to feel or to comprehend that love is a means of knowing, a means of salvation and therefore a means of fulfillment.　He comes to comprehend that love is knowing, not by reflecting on such a possibility, but by loving, by giving oneself over to one's marvelous fate or destiny which is to become elemental, as stated in «Form without Love»:

> *I loved you. . . I don't know.　I don't know what love is.*
> *I suffered you gloriously like blood itself,*
> *like the painful hammer which gives life and kills.*
>
> *I felt daily that life is death.*
> *I knew what it is to love because I died every day.*
>
> *But I never died.　One does not die.　One dies. . .*
> *One dies on an emptiness, on an unloving shoulder.*
> *On an earth indifferent to the very kiss.*

He does not know what love is; what he does know is that by suffering it, by dying, which is to say by living, he can know what it is to love.　By living or dying or loving he comes to know himself.　His existence would be a useless vacumm if he did not love.　The blood which loves and the hammer which kills are on the same symbolic level.　Death (unloving) is found only in an emptiness, on a sterile shoulder or on an indifferent world which ignores the dimension of a kiss.　Time is introduced to intensify love:　«I felt *daily* that life is death./　I knew what it is to love because I died *every day* (italics mine).» As a result, love comes to be a means of salvation when death or the indifferent world which is «burning up» becomes an immediate threat to the being. This is one of the underlying concepts of «Final Fire.» In this poem, «the hope of living yet» is the «little girl small or sweet» with whom the self desires to unite in one single light or «swords in the shadow which motionless will burn up, / will melt united when the flames come.» The world aflame which groans and perishes is paradoxically the salvation of the lovers because in their almost mystical union they create a new fusion or unity of loving transubstantiation: that of the sword which melts united.

Besides the concept of love as a means of knowledge and salvation, there are other conceptual components. On the one hand, there is the mysterious transformation of love into negative death with the concommitant metaphysical melancholy of the poet because of this change; on the other hand, there is the indifference of the world to the presence of and even to the call of love which requires the being to love. The disconsolate poet becomes irritated in the face of the indolent heart which does not respond. The complexity which these components add to the thematic vision of the book derives from the antithetical nature of love which comes, meets the lover, and abandons him, and from the love which, in coming, invites and is ignored by the lover. Furthermore, there is a painful double tension which is inferred from the conflict underlying each conceptual component within itself and from the antithetical relationship with each other: love comes, possesses the being and then abandons him; love comes and the being does not respond. This tension is one of the internal forces which forges the bitter and pessimistic character of *World Alone.*

The poems which develop the first thematic aspect or component are «Form without Love,» «Storm of Love,» «Angry Love,» and «Human Burning»; those which develop the second one are «Edge of Love» and «To Love.»(8) Among the poems of the first group «Angry Love» adds a new twist to the poet's insistence on love when it is discovered that «she» is the destructive «light and darkness»:

> You were the light; the anger, the blood, the cruelty, the
> > lie you were.
> You, life which creaks in the bones,

> *flowers, sending forth by fistfuls their aromas.*
> *Birds that enter through the eyes and blind*
> *the man, nude upon the earth, who looks.*

But the lie he discovers in her will not overcome him; to the contrary, he will continue forward with greater impetus as if trying to redeem her and exalt his own self:

> *I love you; I loved you, I loved you!*
> *I have loved you.*
> *I shall love you the way the body without skin bleeds,*
> *like the last pure stripping of the flesh*
> *that feeds the rivers reddened by anger.*

It is important to point out that the negative character of this poem is suggested in its first lines: «I loved you the way one loves the furious light of a vibrant noon,/ summer that hurts like a red whip.» It is the same whip which at the end will leave him without skin but insisting in his loving desire.(9) In comparison with this desperate situation, in «To Love» he goes on to lament the indifference and the indolence of the world's silence toward love which invites:

> *But you came imitating the simple quiet of the Mountain.*
> *You came the way the warm feather falls from a shaken sky.*
> *The way a rose grows in blind hands.*
> *The way a bird spurts from an adored mouth.*
> *Just like a heart beats against another breast.*

The sweet, tender, cosmic elementalness of love which has just arrived is supreme. The metaphors the poet uses to capture the nature of love and its manner of coming are effective: the mountain, the feather, the rose, the bird and the heart. All suggest elementalness and variety which are joined into one single loving unit. How does it come? Like the simple peace and quiet of the mountain, like the smooth and slow falling of the feather, like the sudden bursting forth of a bird and like the quick beating of a loving heart upon another. But this whole gift of loving grace will be ignored by man: «No one, no one knows you, oh Love, who arrive by a silence ladder,/ by a road from another land invisible.» But the poet transcends this ignorance and states clearly: «I felt you, I saw you, I divined you.» He cannot be confused with the rest which is a formless mass, deaf to the outcry of the blood. From this point of view, love turns into the most effective means for the poet's individual affirmation and fulfillment as a man and as an artist:

B) *The cosmos.* In *World Alone* Aleixandre presents the cosmos as a refuge for the being who flees the indifferent world which, like Nineveh, burns sulphuriously, and also is the painful echo or reflection of the human void. The cosmic refuge can be 1) up above as described in «The Skies,» «Smoke and Earth,» «Birds without Descent,» «The Victorious Sun» and «Celestial Freedom,» whose last strophe reads.:

> *Round clear sky in which to live flying,*
> *in which to sing fluttering eyes that shine,*
> *in which to feel blood like blue firmament*
> *that circulates joyously copying free worlds!*

Up above one lives, one sings, one feels; the being circulates freely like blood. In «Smoke and Earth,» he makes the same reference but with a painful reserve in his soul:

> *I am the* trace of an ended pain.
> *I am the greeting to the purest atmosphere,*
> *to that transparent blue which like one single hand*
> *feels a* silent smoke *on its eternal skin.*   (Stress mine)

2) Refuge is found in the depths of the earth, as is suggested in «Under the Earth,» in that:

> *No.   I am the dark shadow which, among the roots of the*
>   *trees*
> *coils like a serpent making music.*
> *A serpent thick like a tree trunk*
> *under earth breathes without imagining the grass.*

At the end, the poet accuses those who live above of not feeling or knowing the destiny of man. 3) Refuge is found in the sea, as expressed in «Birds without Descent» and in «The Skies,» whose title contrasts paradoxically with the content of the poem in that the sea, not the sky, is exalted:

> *Robust the sea rises without wings to love you,*
> *oh gradual sky where no one has lived.*
> ....
> *Robust, alien, like a Titan it holds up*
> *a whole sky or a breast of love in its arms.*

The poet also laments because man without love, indifferent, does not feel the presence of this refuge. This he does in one of the most beautiful and expressive stanzas of «Birds without Descent»:

> *That is why, stretched out here, on the beach.*
> *Stretched out there afterwards on the hard road.*
> *Stretched out beyond, on the enormous mountain,*
> *a man is unaware of the kind green of the seas,*
> *he is unaware of its melodious and empty surf*
> *and he does not know the eternal cannon of its foam.*

Besides his own lament, he has the sea punish the man by casting him far away: here on the beach, there on the road, and beyond on the mountain. By using the adverbs here, there, beyond, the sea's rejection becomes visualized.

   3) The last cosmic refuge is the breast of the east, stated in «Inhuman World»:

> *Everything flies ceaselessly on the way to the east,*
> *on the way to the fast air towards the breast.*
> *There there are no birds but the clouds roll on*
> *as cautious as the foam of a total ocean.*
>
> *There, there, among the clear joys*
> *of that blue unknown by mortal men,*

The poetic vision derives from the perspective of the western light through which everything flies toward the east, that is, toward the breast of the night unfelt by man.

   If the poet takes pleasure in discovering these cosmic refuges (the breast of the heavens, of the earth, of the sea and of the night), at the same time he feels a great solitude because of the absence of the world which he imagines in the distance from his refuge.   In itself, the refuge is not a total communion.   Thus, in that east which is the night, «there beats a sea which is not blood.»   In the breast of the earth it is not possible to imagine the life above; it is not perceived that «up above and free their petals / are pink, yellow, carmin or innocent.»   In the sea, life means only «an unstable flash, / deep darkness for a single breast.»   If the air is «greeting to the purest atmosphere,» it is also «the trace of an ended pain» or a «silent smoke.»   This tension is another one of the internal forces which makes this book bitter, as clearly indicated in the title itself: *World Alone.*

Having examined the theme of the cosmos as a refuge for the being who flees the indifferent and unloving world, we must study the cosmos as an echo or a reflection of the emptiness of the world. Like this empty world, natural elements also manifest coldness and indifference toward love and life.   «Guitar or Moon,» «It Is No Longer Possible» and «Fallen Moon» are the poems which typify this attitude.   In the latter:

> *the moon, trackless, rolls like doubt,*
> *imitating a pain, a farewell to kisses,*
> *imitating a sadness revealed by dropping the head on the*
> > *breast,*
> *feigning that lilly torn off by the wind.*

the moon feigns a pain it has never felt.   It is a «terrible eye that does not shine, / because it looks within, abyss of the night, / the way dull steel that rolls looks.»   The moon is a lie, a void «like a severed hand / which held in its fingers a broken ring.» All of the linguistic elements which make up this composition accumulate to express sharply the same negative idea; the same impact is felt in «It Is No Longer Possible.»   Here, the poet's pain and anger overflow to such a degree that he says «let the moon roll through the stones of the sky / like an already dead arm without an inflamed rose.»   Man and moon are placed on the same conceptual and symbolic level:

> *But the moon is a bare bone with no accent.*
> *It is not a voice, it is not a celestial cry.*
> *It is its hard hollow, a wall where they resounded,*
> *thick walls where the sound of kisses used to break.*

In the moon, the memories of a dead love only echo. Most likely these were the poems which led the critics to oversimplify the complexity and the importance of this book.

C) *Man.* Following our analysis of love and the cosmos, little remains to be said about man, given that the study of the former themes involved the study of man. Still, this is the thematic course most decried by the critics who, basing themselves on such obvious poems as «Man Doesn't Exist» (the first in the book), «Inhuman World» and «Nobody», concluded that the work was pessimistic without examining the complexity of it. What is important is to discover why and how it is pessimistic. Aleixandre's visionary world in this book is not merely a pessimistic outcry. Each poem presents a variation of the same symphony of despair; each piece comprises an expansion which complements contradicts, questions, and endows the whole with a vital and artistic complexity.

II

Having studied the three thematic visions of *World Alone,* it is necessary now to analyze the technical elaboration of these themes, especially the various metaphoric forms and their effects.

A) *Metaphoric contrasts.* Frequently there appears at the beginning and end of the poem a chain of metaphors which through their poetic and real nature contrast with each other to such a degree that they seem to negate each other. The purpose is clear: to express the painful tension of the poet facing his intuition of the vision and to instill in the reader the unresolvable doubt inherent in the intuition. The first and next-to-last strophes of «Human Burning» exemplify this tension:

> *Calm ship which floats along a river,*
> *at times I wonder if your body is a bird.*
> *At times if it is water, water or the river itself;*
> *but always I embrace you like a voice between lips.*
> ....
> *But you who rest here the way light rests on a summer*

> *afternoon,*
> *you are proud like nakedness without trees,*
> *violent like the reddened moon*
> *and burning like the river evaporated by a volcano.*

In the first strophe, her loving serenity and calm are what fascinate
and confuse the poet: She is «a calm ship,» «bird,» «water,»
«river,» «voice between lips.»   These five metaphors are so inter-
related that they lose their individuality and forge one single idea
and emotion: peace and innocence.   The elemental nature of
the bird, the water, the river and the voice is transmitted to
the ship turning it into a cosmic element.   Although the ship
is a product of man, the imagery makes it elemental through its
contact with the calm the other images suggest.

To present a conceptual and an emotional antithesis, in the
ending strophe, the beloved is the opposite: proud, violent and
inflamed.   These negative qualities stated in a first degree of a
comparison will be raised to a second degree of intensity so that
the contrast with the former calm becomes sharper.   Her pride
is compared with the treeless nakedness: sterile, monotonous,
egocentric earth.   Her violence is not loving but sterile like the
anger of the «reddened moon.»   This is not the desired and loving
violence which is perceived, for example, in «To Love»:   «violent
like doves who love,/ cooing like those beasts unextinguished
by a sunset.»   Here it is uselessly inflamed like a river full of
lava and smoke which, in contrast with the first river, cannot be
navigated.   The clarity and innocence of the first river reflects the
clarity and innocence of the water.   The second, however, has lost
even its river-qualities.   The smooth serene rhythm of the first
lines contrasts with the brusk irregularity of the end lines.   In
sum, these are the antitheses which create the painful tension of
this poem.   It is importan to point out that the «but» in the next-
to-the-last strophe differs from the «but» which begins the last
one: the first suggests the poet's confusion because of the
change in his beloved, the second, resignation.

B)   *Metaphoric layering.*   Although this technical device is not,
of course, exclusive to Aleixandre, it is important to explore how
he uses it and what its effects are and herein lies his originality.
This device is also typical of the Generation of '27 and of 17the century Spanish poetry.   What happens with this linguistic device is

that, using A. I. Richard's terminology, the vehicle of the first
figurative level, becomes the tenor of the second; the vehicle of the
second, in turn, becomes the tenor of the third which, in order to
express it, has introduced a new vehicle.(10)   The poet says in
«Under the Earth»:

> *No.   I am the dark shadow which, among the roots*
> *of the trees*
> *coils like a serpent making music.*
> *A serpent thick like a tree trunk*
> *under earth breathes without imagining the grass.*(11)

There is a linking together of three metaphors whose tenors
are transformed into vehicles in order to lead into the following
figurative level. 1)   The being is like the shadow which goes
through the roots of trees.   The idea of life begins to emerge
because of the direct association of the shadow with the roots,
the dark shadow ceases being that and becomes paradoxically
luminous. 2)   The shadow is like a musical serpent; that is, it
has overcome the silence of the shadow.   Furthermore,its vitality
is communicated by means of music. 3)   The musical serpent is
thick like a trunk which breathes in order to nourish the tree.
Again vitality is communicated.   The two extremes, the *being* and
the *tree,* expressed by a chain of transmitting metaphors, form a
vital cycle.   This chain is particularly reinforced by the long
presence of the serpent which carries life from the *being* to the
tree.   Each metaphor linked to the previous one interconnects all
the lines and, similarly, makes the entire strophe a continuous
communication of life and love.   The effect of this metaphoric
layering produces an artistic and a conceptual pleasure.   Hence,
its unique use is original.   It is not a mere technical virtuosity
on the part of Aleixandre, but rather a necessary form of expression.   This uninterrupted communication of life required such
layering so that each level introduces into the next its tenor
to be converted into a vehicle and thus continue the figurative
layering.

C)   *Metaphoric proliferation.*   Aleixandre's poetry and especially his first period is primarily characterized by its imaginative
force which pours forth with effusion--and with great artistic
control--an abundance of metaphors.   This is a typical of *Destruc-*

tion or Love, Swords like Lips (both before *World Alone*), and in
Shadow of Paradise (after *World Alone*) it diminishes without
disappearing altogether. This technique is still widely utilized
in *World Alone;*(12) as exemplified in «Birds without Descent»:

> *A blonde hair waves.*
> *Remote beaches can be seen, happy clouds, a wind so golden*
> *That it would connect bodies on the pure sand.*
> *Birds without descent flee through the blue.*
> *They are almost desires, they are almost foam.*
> *They are the leaves of a sky radiant with beauty,*
> *where a thousand throats sing light without death.*

In this stanza which seems a whole poem in itself (notice the beginning, the development, and the conclusion) there are eleven
independent and complementary metaphors: blonde hair
(rays of the sun), light, desires, clouds, beaches, wind, sand,
birds, foam, leaves, skies and a thousand throats (the musical
birds). All are or allude to cosmic elements. Together with this
elemental concert which the poet perceives in the radiant skies
of any day are also suggested positive elemental states: freedom,
love and life. The free verse and the quickness of its rhythm
underline the content. One feels that the poet has let his flock
of metaphors fly free through the sky of the poem. His
enthusiasm in the presence of this elemental and loving world is
evident in the overflowing spirit of his metaphoric creation;
indeed the metaphoric profusion which is the expression or reflection of the profusion of cosmic elements creates the artistic unity
which is similarly the reflection of the loving unity of the sky in the
poem. It is important to add that when the poet says that from
the sky «remote beaches can be seen,» there is suggested a fusion
of the sky with the sea creating another elemental union. On
those beaches, the poet imagines that the «golden» wind would
fuse, «would connect [loving] bodies on the pure sand.» The
fusion of sky and sea is expressed with the «music of a thousand
throats which «sing light without death.» The verbs linking
these metaphors, to wave, to connect, to flee, to sing, are a projection of cosmic freedom and joy; the adjectives, blonde, golden,
pure, radiant, pursue the same celestial clarity.

This has been a love poem, but the same metaphoric formula
is used by the poet to express his anger and disconcertion facing

the opposite situation, as is the case in «Fallen Moon,» «Nobody» and «Man Does Not Exist.» What is ironic about the last poem is that it is precisely the moon, a vacuum in itself, that goes seeking man, another vacuum. From the metaphoric configuration of the poem, it is inferred that the more places the moon goes looking for the being, the more intensely the vacuum is felt. With the very same purpose the author, with thirty-five verbs of action (excluding the verb *to be*), gives the poem the proper sense of dynamism to capture the moon's mobility.

D) *Metaphoric expansion.* This device consists of the repeated and developed association of words which have to do, directly or indirectly, with the vehicle or tenor of the poem's central metaphor. We study it here because it is a device which requires great structural concentration and also because *World Alone* is a surrealist work. Indeed the author included thirteen poems from this book in his anthology of *Surrealist Poetry.*(13) There are many poems which exemplify this phenomenon. In «The Tree,» the tenor is man, and therefore the other metaphors with which the poem is constructed are; leg, thigh, knee, muscles, arm, veins, blood, heart and eyes. The purpose? Not only to humanize the tree, but to make it take the place of man. Thus the human being is supplanted by the tree. Only at the end does the poem take an unexpected turn when the tree «never cries out/ nor does it ever cast its shadow on mortal men.» This is its defect. Through expansion, the poem becomes a coherent, emotional, visual and conceptual experience in which the tree is transformed into a human reality. This technique will be further studied in «Form without Love» at the end of this chapter.

E) *Metaphoric dynamism.* (*World Alone* is a link between the first and the second poetic periods of Aleixandre). This device, very typical of the second stage, consists of a gradual internal movement of the poem's structure. In the case of «The Tree,» the metaphoric dynamism reinforces the poetic construction of creation of the tree in human terms. One can actually see the poet, like a god, constructing the tree from the base of its trunk up to the top of its branches. Having finished, he proudly contemplates his creation.

In «Under the Earth,» the poet resorts to the same method to suggest a dynamism of inverse direction. That is, the poetic vision moves from the first subterranean level to the soil itself penetrating its deepest and most hidden strata. Notice the careful use of certain key words which the poet selects precisely for this effect. These words are underlined in the following lines: «*Under* earth one lives, the moisture is blood»; «*Beneath* the earth there exists *deeper,* the rock»; «There is water *under* the earth»; «*Deeper, deeper,* fire purifies.» It is as if the poet were taking his reader on a flight through the deepest inwards of the earth, uncovering them to the world: the rock, the water, and the fire which «purifies,» a verb which endows the journey with a religious or mystical tone. In these compositions, one feels how the dynamic structure of the poem reflects the dynamic desire of the poet which erects the three and which penetrates deeper and deeper into the earth.

In Aleixandre's poetic evolution, the use of this device becomes increasingly accentuated, starting with *Destruction or Love* until it becomes typical in *History of the Heart.* Hence, *World Alone* connects the two stages. It evolves together with the gradual poetic de-hermeticization of Aleixandre. Also visible in this evolution is the diminishing use of the conjunction «or.» In *World Alone* there are approximately fifty identifiable uses of «or» in comparison with the two hundred in *Destruction or Love* and the ten or twelve in *Shadow of Paradise.*(14) There are groups of negative formulas which, instead of negating, affirm. These do not exist in *Destruction or Love*; there are few of them in *World Alone*; and they abound in *Shadow of Paradise.* This indicates that *World Alone* is stylistically a link between the two books.

F) *Metaphoric development in «Form without Love.»* Having examined the principal technical characteristics of *World Alone,* it is appropriate to analyze a typical poem in order to comprehend more throughly the effects which the various stylistic and metaphoric devices produce in the whole of Aleixandre's production. It is also important to analyze the various internal and external shades of structure and the gradual evolution of the intuition throughout the poem. The poem chosen for this purpose is «Form without Love,» which has forty-two lines. Its external and internal structure permits a division into eight poetic moments:(15)

1. Line 1: With the emphatic «Enough, sadness, enough,

enough, enough» there is as much evidence of sorrow because that body no longer loves as there is evidence of disgust because of the persistence of the sorrow. This moment presents the powerful psychological tension between wanting and not wanting to forget that loveless body.

2.   Lines 2-4:   The poet states that it is necessary to think no more of the eyes, or of the forehead, or of the beloved's blonde hair.   The focus is on the luminousness of her face, the clarity with which he fell in love and which he now desires to cast aside. He is convinced about what he wants to do: abandon her.

3.   Lines 5-8:   But how to do it if he remembers the moment when he first possessed her, when he drank in light or sweet blood from her veins?   Here, love is pain or sorrow; not an empty but a vital pain.   This third moment negates the decision to abandon her stated in the second.   Consequently the tension goes on tearing apart his being.

4.   Lines 9-16:   This moment is a reflection on the nature of the love he is suffering.   He cannot define it rationally with logical formulas.   But he does know what it is because of what he feels. Loving is dying every day.   Dying is living.   One only dies, one is only empty, when one does not love, when one does not live. He who lives and does not love is dead.   This is the philosophical basis of *World Alone.*

5.   Lines 17-190:   He keeps on reliving her: «Your were so tender...» «sweet as the wind in the leaves/ like a mound of roses for fixed lips.»   He makes her elemental by associating her with the wind and the roses.   Connecting the «there» of line 17 with the «mound of roses» in line 19, the image of her body stretched out is suggested.   This is the ideal posture described in many other poems in this book (for example in «Edge of Love»).   It is, besides, a natural, unarranged heap.   In «Edge of Love» she will be a «mound of nubile wheat.»   The wind and the roses are sweet because of the smoothness felt both on the leaves and on the lips.   Notice the calmness and the delicacy of this crucial moment in the development of the inner world of the poet and his total surrender to his remote happiness.

6. Lines 20-28: The initial adverb «afterwards» introduces the unexpected and mysterious cause of her change into a form without love. «A vengeful flash, some enigmatic destiny» fell upon love, extinguishing it. There is not a clear reason. Through the metaphoric expansion the whole strophe acquires a dark tonality which corresponds with the death of her as a lover: «vengeful flash,» «cursed light,» «stormy sky,» «purple lightening.» This fatal flash struck her face: eyes and forehead, the very same features he refused to think about in moment 2. The evocation continues. The poet goes on reliving those happy and painful moments. At the same time he seeks relief, he wounds himself.

7. Lines 25-28: The initial conjunction «and» likewise suggests what that explosion of evil did to her: the center of hatred and death. Her clear loving eyes now are «phosphorous» red eyes which glare hatred toward the heavens and the mountains which now are barren and sterile.

8. Lines 29-38: «Who are you? What face is that, what diamond hardness?/ What marble reddened by the storm/ unappeased by kisses or by sweet memory?» These are the questions with which this strophe erupts. No longer is it a matter of an evocation. The poet now confronts his present and hers. Because of the change, she is unknowable. He perceives that a transformation he cannot comprehend has occurred. That sweet «mound of roses» which represented her body surrendered to his lips in moment 5 has been turned into «reddened marble» and «a stone rose without blood» by the purple lightening. Now water and kisses slide off her marble body and the poet feels that kissing her is only kissing his own anguish and his own tears.

9. Lines 39-42: He does not cast her off. To the contrary, he embraces her knowing well that the body is a stone, a rock, a hard mountain, a dead body from which he seeks death. This moment expresses the metaphysical confusion of the poet who, having reviewed the history of his love, ends up asking for his own death. The various moments of this poem correspond to the different moods of the poet, who, reliving his past with the purpose of freeing himself from pain or sorrow, enters into his present reality even more confused than before. The dynamism is appropriate

to the poet's gradual discovery of his inner world, memory by memory, until he arrives at the only possible conclusion from an esthetic and emotional point of view.

World Alone, as was stated at the beginning of this essay, has suffered because of non-literary circumstances. They have directly affected its dissemination, popularity and the proper appreciation of its importance in the development of Aleixandre's first period. Regardless of what Aleixandre said, both thematically and stylistically, this book marks the transition between *Destruction or Love* and *Shadow of Paradise.* After completing *Destruction or Love,* what Aleixandre does in *World Alone* is focus his elemental cosmic vision from the perspective of the absent love. This aspect was defined already in several poems in the earlier book and what he does in the new one is carry this aspect to its final consequences. Furthermore, *World Alone* forces the poet to take, as a subsequent intuition, another step in his evolution toward what is expressed in *Shadow of Paradise* where, after having submerged himself in the depths of an indifferent and loveless world, he seeks the new paradisiacal light of childhood in a new world in which the being is affirmed and fulfilled as a loving and participating entity of the universe. The poet sings this world not with the surrealistic emphasis of his earlier works, but with a new, less hermetic diction no less effective than his earlier diction. This de-hermeticization becomes apparent in *World Alone.* In synthesis, the three moments of Aleixandre's evolutionary vision and creation are: loving destruction is life, in *Destruction or Love;* loveless destruction is death, in *World Alone;* from death the impetus to sing the new light of paradise will be reborn in *Shadow of Paradise.*

NOTES

1. *Ambit* and *Ultimate Birth* are intentionally excluded from this group because

of the immaturity and artificiality of the first and because of the lack of structural unity of the second.

2. It is interesting to note in Aleixandrine bibliography the preponderance of critical studies of the first period (*Passion of the Earth*, 1928, to *Shadow of Paradise*, 1944).

3. Eugenio de Nora, *Mundo a solas*, *Correo literario*, Año I (June 1, 1950), p. 10.

4. Aleixandre, *Obras completas*, 1968, pp. 1451-1452.

5. Aleixandre, *Obras completas*, 1968, p. 1451.

6. Aleixandre, *Obras completas*, 1968, p. 1471.

7. Carlos Bousoño, «Un nuevo libro de Aleixandre: *Mundo a solas*,» *Insula*, Núm. 53 (May 15, 1950), p. 2.

8. There are seven poems devoted entirely to «love.» The study of «Final Fire» shows how the poet trusts in it for his salvation.

9. At the end of this chapter, when we study «Form without Love» from the point of view of technique, the clear development of this will become apparent.

10. Vicente Cabrera, *Tres poetas a la luz de la metáfora: Salinas, Aleixandre y Guillén*, (Madrid: Gredos, 1975), pp. 134-137.

11. We shall return to «Under the Earth» to examine in more detail the second part.

12. Cabrera, *Tres poetas*, pp. 125-131.

13. Vicente Aleixandre, *Poesía surrealista* (Barcelona: Barral, 1971). The author states in his preliminary note: «This irrationalist sequence is the one I have tried to represent in this anthology. The greatest contribution is made by the works closest to strictly defined surrealism (from *Passion of the Earth* to *World Alone*).»

14. The approximate number of occurrences of «or» in *World Alone* are by my own count; Carlos Bousoño counts the «or» in *Destruction or Love* and *Shadow of Paradise*. *La poesía de Vicente Aleixandre*, 3rd. ed. (Madrid: Gredos, 1968), p. 329.

15. See the poem in the last section of this book.

POEMS OF CONSUMMATION

José Olivio Jiménez
Hunter College

Poems of Consummation is structured around a fundamental theme which, when formulated, permits at least two possible statements. One of them would be an exaltation of and an elegy for youth: exaltation because youth is proclaimed as the only valuable reality in the voratious vertigo of existence; elegy because this proclamation is made precisely when that reality, youth, can be contemplated only as totally lost. The other aspect of the theme, more general and diluted but inextricable from the former, is the diagnosis of what living has been; a diagnosis made from that peak of human temporality, old age, when because of the accumulation of human experience, man has arrived at his maximum, and simultaneously most useless, wisdom. But this general thematic center which must be reconstructed after the necessary rational explanation given above, has not risen from any aspiration to generous moral utopias, nor from any of those cosmic impulses habitual in Aleixandre which reveal in his work a healthy ethical, intellectual or imaginative vitality. It is well known that the author has constructed many of his other poetic works according to such a design, starting with the brilliant mystical-pantheistic conception of *Destruction or Love,* to the comforting theory of time as the integrator of the theme developed in *In a Vast Dominion,* to mention only two very different works in Aleixandre's development.(1) On the other hand, it could be said that *Poems of Consummation* was born from an imminent biographical situation: the poet's age, and either directly or indirectly, this situation informs the spirit of all the poems and from it emanates the immediacy, the authenticity and the sincerity, the absolute lyricism of the book. In fact, it is now the untransferable man within the poet, the one who contemplates his own youth as very distant, as the only time full of meaning for one who, like Aleixandre, has been an impassioned glorifier of

71

matter in its limpid natural vigor, and who now, on the other side, finds himself facing the only remaining truth, Death, and is capable of dignifying the prolonged deceit of worn-out existence. By virtue of the implacable power of this vision, the point of view from which these poems have been conceived is painful.(2)

Aleixandre has had the daring to enter, with no attenuating illusions, into the dramatic problem which tears apart an old man still anxious to prove his love of life. And upon doing this, he may well have provided an escape for his present inner demon in a kind of poetic-moral exorcism which will leave him cleansed and prepared for the new and more audacious adventures in thought of which his next book, *Dialogues of Knowledge,* is the best proof. On turning to this theme, what Aleixandre does in *Poems of Consummation* is articulate this poetry of his maturity congruently with that of his earlier maturity: *In a Vast Dominion,* or with the earlier *Shadow of Paradise,* or even with the poetry of his shaken youth, *Destruction or Love.* Throughout all of his works, he had enthusiasticaly sung the identification of man with natural reality; to achieve this in all of its intensity required that it be intuited in terms of energy, force and brillance: attributes exclusive to youth. Nature, as a moral lesson to be imitated or as an attracting force to any dream of pantheistic union, manifests itself solely in the form of vital force, operative, perpetually renovated and totally free of any sign of decadence or annihilation. What happens now is that the poet, because of his personal circumstance and moment (present old-age, lost youth), has decided to treat historically what has always been the core of his poetry; although certain earlier periods, like the one of *History of the Heart,* responded to a projection of meaning analogous to what is suggested here. These circumstances will determine the inevitable elegiac tone, since the one who suffers them cannot forget that at one time his own youth and the plenitude of nature were the same thing and this explains the heart-rending side of many of these poems. But the years have also brought serenity, that is, the state of mind necessary to examine what is remaining of human existence, what of him will remain as true substance and singular destiny. This examination, calm and melancholy, reflective and pathetic, will reveal the other face of the book, constructive and enriching, and will give it its depth and universality.

Poems of Consummation opens with the intentionally objective presentation of its hero (or antihero) and of his situation, the situation of the mature man on the way to his end.   This man is already protected from life, exiled from it, by an opaque cortex-- his age; thus from the beginning he is depicted with insistence on this opprobrious protection, as expressed in «The Years»:

> But the years cast
> something like a turbid round clarity,
> and he moves within the hated globe.   And
> he is not visible
> or he scarcely is, because he passes by unknown
> and stays enveloped.

Nevertheless, this man stays aware and sensitive to the physical beauty which in very concrete forms continues to flourish in those places where his now slowed steps take him, and this produces the greatest pain:

> ...Because the eye--which is still alive--looks
> and copies the gold of the hair, the rosy flesh,
> the white of the sudden ivory.   The laughter
> is clear
> to everyone, and also to him, who lives and hears it.

The first poems carefully delineate the spiritual situation of the old man: his being now made up solely of memory, the opposition between his sterile wisdom and the vital ignorance or indiference of the young, and the existential disbelief provoked by his awareness of consummation.   And when dazzled by the brilliance of that which still envigorates with splendor, he notices in contrast the deteriorization precipitated by old age, still he would dare to portray physical senility with its most fragile features (as in «Final Face,» to be commented on later).

As the book proceeds even up to its end, he insists with increasing subjectivity, and overcoming the initial objectivization, on the personal reactions of the older man in the face of what has been his life.   The elegy, without becoming altogether lost, gradually gives way to the location and analysis of the hard truths discovered by a human being who emotionally rationalized his own old age and existence itself.(3)   Here follows a summary, with some textual examples, of these painful discoveries: the need to avoid memory if nothing persists, as in «The past: Pure village»:

> *To wake.   To live.   I*
> *cannot,*
> *I ought not*
> *remember.   Nothing lives.   Curtain which the wind moves*
> *without existing.   And I am silent.*

The recognition of doubt, solitude, oblivion and ignorance as the only sad possessions of existence and, in the face of all that, that death is the only absolute knowledge of man: «Not to know is living.   To know, dying it» («Yesterday»); «To doubt. . .?   The one who doubts, exists.   Only dying is knowledge» («Without Faith»).   And in spite of everything, the unappeasing appetite for knowing has formed the base of Aleixandre's poetic necessity. Clear distinction is made between «known,» an inferior acquisition, tangible and therefore possible, and true «knowing,» supreme and total aspiration and, because of the very nature of the ambition, unattainable.   The almost aphoristic passages which exemplify this distinction abound in the book: «To live a lot is dark, and suddenly to know is not knowing oneself» («A Few Words»); «To know is knowing?   I am not knowing you and I knew («Without Faith»); «Knowing is not the same as to know» («A Term»); «Man doubts./   The old man knows.   Only the child is knowing» («The Comet»).   In relation to this objective of final knowledge, a prudent precaution is not to trust in the senses, the fallacious mediaries of reality: «The one who sees is deceived/ the one who does not look is knowing» («You are Waiting»).   And since the data of the senses merely establish a phantasmagorical setting, it is also useful to mistrust memory, a different form of vain illusionism or unreality, stated in «Near to Death»:

> *The majesty of memory is air*
> *afterwards, or before.   Facts are a sigh.*
> *That curtain of yellow silk*
> *that a breath moves, and another light puts out.*

Against such a sombre background, the two positive elements of the book stand out luminously.   One, youth, although sacrilegiously amputated by time, is the only certain and indubitable reality: «Do not insist. Youth does not deceive. It shines by itself» («Limit and Mirror»); «Life. Life is being young and nothing more» («He Doesn't Know It»). The other is love which, more than being a theme in these poems, impregnates them like an exultant and vivifying act of faith. Within the chaos and devastation of living, love offers one possible form of survival: «Your deceased lips suggest to me/ that I live.» («Present, Afterwards»). Love offers a harmonious integration of opposites: «A unity of the day when, in love, it was night» («Song of Nocturnal Day»), and of a redeeming concretion of the being in the presence of the resistant beloved body: «You, my limitation, my dream. Be!» («The Limit»).

Before concluding these considerations which, broadly speaking, deal with the content of the book, we should stress that at the very center of the book there is a whole section which represents an opening up of the basic central theme. More precisely, the poems of this section present an integration of the personal or lyric opposition with the maximum implications this problem can generate on a universal scale. The absorbed look within which sets the tone of *Poems of Consummation* once again moves toward the cosmos and towards history, the two horizons the poet envisioned in the two earlier stages of his poetic production which are, respectively, the raison d'etre of *Destruction or Love* and *History of the Heart*. But now the nature of this impulse undergoes a pronounced refinement which defines the most characteristic and transcendental part of his current phase. The poet will no longer place such emphasis on the demarcation or the identification of the I with the physical or historical cosmos, the well-known aleixandrine utopias, but rather on the possibility for man to achieve some valid form of objective and universal certitude. This obsession for knowing previously referred to, will gain prominence with this part of *Poems of Consummation* and continue into *Dialogues of Knowledge,* giving substance to a fundamental question which condenses this gnostic concern essential to Aleixandre's new period. This question could be stated thus: is pure thought sufficient? That which exists in the solipsistic form of the creature-merely-thought? The answer is dual as it always has been since the most ancient philosophical inquiries in the history of western culture; and from it derive the apparent epistemological contradictions of the poems. From the

existential point of view, it is not sufficient: «Thought alone is
not visible,» he writes in the poem «The One Who Was.» From
the metaphysical angle, however, it is the only category that can
be accepted, and at times, as in «The Young,» it even stands as
the greatest possible beauty, the beauty of pure thought in its
intangible reality:

> *...The light*
> *stays happy, ah, not touched,*
> *because*
> *the one who wasn't born doesn't stain.   Everything*
> *   lights,*
> *believed: oh immaculate thought.*
> *Beautiful, like the intact thought alone:*
> *a glimmer.*

In this central section there are passages that catch us like
hallucinating bursts of wind.   Salvador de Madariaga has some-
where written: «Just as an excess of light dazzles and blinds,
so excessive reality leads to hallucination.»   This is what happens
in these particular poems now intimately open to the world.   The
old man, lucid protagonist of the adventure of the book, by pres-
sing his own crisis of being, his ontological reality, into a universal
projection, tends either to eliminate or to enlarge the strictly
rational limits of things and words and to use this verbal and visual
hypertension to suggest the cosmic apocalypse of all creation;
as can be seen in «If Anyone Had Told Me»:

> *A long time ago the cold*
> *had a birthday.   The moon slipped into waters.*
> *The sea closed up, and turned green in its brilliance.*
> *For a long time, a long long time*
> *it has slept.   The waves become quiet.*
> *The foam sounds the same, only of silence.*
> *It is like a sad fist*
> *and it grabs the dead and explains them,*
> *and shakes them, and bashes them agains the*
> *   fierce rocks*

The strict subjectivity and the lucidity of vision and language are
not lost, however, and he returns to them immediately.   The

poem that closes the book, «Oblivion,» ends like this:

> *It is and was not, but it was and is silent.*
> *The cold burns and in your eyes is born*
> *its memory.   To remember is obscene;*
> *worse: it is sad.   To forget is to die.*
>
> *With dignity it died.   Its shadow crosses.*

These are lines which manifest with the greatest possible serious-
ness the sustained expressive and spiritual force of the book:
a semi-definition of the pathetic moral urgency that inspired it.

The above comments allow us now to contemplate *Poems of
Consummation* as what it is in its unity: a vast poetic symbol with
an inner structure of thought which turns on a primary central
axis, most notably on the temporal poles of youth--old age and
their many possible and varied amplifications or reductions (such
as knowledge--ignorance; existential reality--idealism; presence--
oblivion; plenitude--vacuum; immanence--transcendence, etc.),
leading up to the ultimate and definitive set which will dissolve
in the fatal equation life--death.   But on unraveling these polar
matrices, there gradually appear diverse modules of expression
which, when developed, come to the point where their pristine
sense of opposition is completely extinguished.   The simplest
of these mechanisms has a static enunciative character: merely
to oppose the signs of youth, fresh and blinding brilliance, vital
indifference, with the signs of old age, the darkness of the years
and a pathetic awareness of reality.   A more developed form will
make the polar elements coincide, those elements which necessarily coexist in the process of the dissolution of being into
nothingness which is living.   An example of this occurs in «The
Old Man Is Like Moses,» where in an attempt to define dying,
contrary images of ending and fulfilling are juxtaposed:

> *To die one sunset is enough.*
> *A bit of shadow on the line of the horizon.*
> *A swarming of adolescences, hopes, voices.*
> *And there, succession, earth: the limit.*
> *What the others will see.*

And lastly there is one more violent technique of confrontation which makes equal or which fuses the opposite terms. it could almost be an exercise in dialectics in the truest Hegelian sense but transformed into poetry. The two explicit, counterpoised concepts would be the thesis and the antithesis; the synthesis, implicit, nullifying and therefore poetic, is the suggestion of nothingness which comes from confounding what had been previously presented in a rational way as distinct and exclusive. An evocative poem, «The Past: Pure Village»: «Everything persists, or dead» identifies in memory the irreducible ideas of survival and destruction. In another place, this poem sketches a desolate and illusory physical and emotional landscape as the backdrop to life. And again two mutually contradictory intuitions come together and fuse: one glimpse of the leaves which fall, a sign of the wornout and decayed, and another glimpse of the new leaves which rise to the tree, a visionary suggestion of possible deception. And these two intuitiions appear mingled, not separated, by means of the same conjunction *or* as in the previous example:

> *The leaves have fallen, or from the earth to the tree*
> *they rose today*
> *and still they feign*
> *passion, being, sound. And I cross*
> *and they give no shade,*
> *since they are. And there is no smoke.*

Observe how in the last two lines the nullifying or undoing opposition is expressed without the use of linking conjuctions: the leaves *are* and at the same time they *give no shade,* when in fact the projections of shade objectively would be one of their manifestations of being in reality.

The poem «Near to Death» accumulates a series of antithetical insinuations so that each time we are about to catch a positive truth we come upon a phrase or a word of diametrically opposite meaning introduced by that ferocious *or* intended to extinguish the glimmer of reality which was suggested in the truncated affirmative clause. This fragment is an example of this technique:

> *It is not sadness that life points to*
> *or nears, when the steps are many, and they last.*
> *There the wilderness, here the glassy city,*

> *or it is a reflection of that very long sun*
> *that plots responses*
> *long distance*
> *for lips that, living, live,*
> *or recall.*
> *The majesty of memory is air*
> *afterwards, or before.*

Facing the imminence of the definitive end, as suggested by the title of the poem, no superior importance is attached to this or that, to the real or the imagined, to the lived or the remembered. From the painfully illuminating perspective of old age, everything dissolves into a general ontological undifferentiation; everything is one and the same. Aleixandre's characteristic, identifying *or*, so well studied by Bousoño, gains here, through the magnitude of the experience it assimilates and expresses, its most nihilistic existential and metaphysical meaning, toward which he had been tending ever since the early period of *Destruction or Love*.

One of the most brilliant and compelling aspects of *Poems of Consummation* is the quality of expression. Although the book emerges from an act of thought (the intellectual penetration of some of the most anguishing and transcendental problems of existence), it in no way slights the sensorial and the affective elements necessary to true poetic expression. What is thought is felt with profound emotion and turned into a symbolic language that rests upon vigorous concrete imagery. For Aleixandre, poetry has always been an intrinsic fact of language; even when he has most laden his verse with feeling or thought, he has not deviated from this premise. Because of the requirement of objective statement, it is in the beginning section of the book where the poet feels the need to round out his symbolic configurations with greater plasticity and deliberateness. A fresh, almost organic sensorialness serves to communicate warm palpitation to the glorious fact of youth and a controlled dynamism to the tense action of living during this phase of impelling but unconscious ascent; as we see in «The Old and the Young»:

> *It is the first greening of the early season.*
> *A youthful river, rather the childhood of a nearby spring,*
> *and the incipient greening; young oaks,*

woods by the port in swift ascent.
Very swift...

But, as is to be expected, he frequently has to resort to images of opposite symbolic value in order to clarify the precise shades of old age. Some of these images represent moments of true expressive mastery. We have already seen the opaque crust of old age described as a «hated globe»; but in the development of this symbol, in «The Years,» the poet comes to indicate how, in spite of everything, the old man who adds nothing to life since he is invisible to everyone else, continues receiving from the external world its most direct stimuli:

He hears and feels, because the strange wall
robs him of his light but air is only
for the light that comes, and passes the edge.

This intermediary step between life and death, old age, caught up in its fatal destiny, will necessarily produce pain but can still give the firm impression of stability if it is sensed according to its instantaneousness and according to its wisdom (regardless of how vain this may prove in the end). Thought also acquires a suggestive poetic form. Facing the unstable youths who move forward with their quick step, the same poem «The Old and the Young» says:

The old look at them. They are still,
these are, the ones who at the end of life,
on the edge of the end, remain suspended,
without falling, as if forever.

Every now and then, the expression becomes literally fleshless. The contemplation of old age also permits an aesthetic sorrow which Aleixandre, always the singer of natural beauty, captures in its finest points. By «aesthetic» we do not suggest anything elaborate or artificial, rather we refer to the kingdom of the beautiful within nature, in contrast to which the disfigured final face of the old man shocks like a blasphemy. The years bring physical decay, the ruin of human matter, which is not the least of its ironic gifts. The poet, in order to leave no gap in his theme, stresses this sad aspect by offering us almost an

X-ray vision of the features that already exhibit the deformed traces of the mercilously destroyed face. The following etching, crudely infrarealistic, comes from «Final Face»:

Because the old man is not his mask, but some other
                                             lewd nakedness;
beyond the skin it is peering out,
without dignity. Disorder: what we see is not a face.
That is why, when the old man exhibits his hilarious vision
                          he sees himself behind bars,
degraded, the recollection of some living, and there appears
the pointed nose, eaten or gnawed away, the thinning hair,
a mat, the turbid drop that makes up the eye, and
                                        the hollow or crack
where the mouth was and is missing. There a dry wound
still opens and mimicks some sound; a sad bellows.
With hooks grasping the bars, sounds broken by
several large yellow teeth are mouthed, which
if they exist, belong to another specie.
                                   No longer human.

This would be very close to the stylization of the *esperpento* if it were not that the universal dimension of the portrait endows the image with an immediate and general pathos which elevates and redeems it poetically.

Having reached the heart of the book, it is no longer indispensable for the poet to elaborate the direct, plastic or symbolic representations with such beauty. They are developed when necessary and some are expanded. For example, the idea that living is a voluntary but in the long run a futile act through which man tries to subvert the inexorable law of existence is poetically developed in «A Term» as follows:

They swim against the current, but they retreat,
and carried in the waters while they struggle upstream,
they end up on their backs.
It is the end with everything into which they sink.

Another example is the representation of the step from full

existence to the pre-death of old age as the transition from sea to foam; as in «If Anyone Had Told Me»:

> *The sea closed up, and turned green in its brilliance.*
> *For a long time, a long long time,*
> *it has slept.   The waves become quiet.*
> *The foam sounds the same, only of silence.*

When poetic necessity dictates, he resorts to elaborations of this kind. But generally speaking, the reader feels as if the lexical and imaginative devices were being gradually reduced, thinning out almost to extinction. What it means is that Aleixander, in the majority of these poems, has achieved the maximum economy of words and hence of concision and intensity in his poetic development. The rhetorical impetus he managed so well so frequently, here seems to diminish: the poem becomes abbreviated, the line tightens, the word is condensed. The impact of this concentration strikes deep, so that at times we cannot discover immediately the subtle virtuosity of language which produces that impact. The virtuosity is there, only so exact and so austere that it seems as if it were hidden in order to let the harsh, naked concept predominate. It is not the concept, however, that strikes us, but the sharp tremor which accompanies reflection. This act of reflection could center on the death--life duality of the poem «The Limit,» but it is the strong underlying emotion that moves us because of the moment in life from which it was written as well as because of the sobre tightness of expression, which makes this one of the most intense love poems composed by Aleixandre:

> *Enough.   It is not insisting to look at the long shining*
>   *of your eyes.   There to the end of the world.*
> *I looked and I obtained.   I contemplated and it was passing.*
> *The dignity of man is in his death.*
> *But the temporary shining adds*
> *color, truth.   The light, once thought, deceives.*
> *Enough.   In the current of light--your eyes--I put*
> *my faith.   Through them I saw, I would live.*
> Today when I tread my end, I kiss these limits.
> *You, my limitation, my dream.   Be!*

In other texts, it is the sensorial coloring that quantitatively seems to dominate the expression. Here we should stress what has previously only been insinuated: throughout the book there is a fundamental opposition, on which the book rests, that systematically relies on symbols of «shadow,» «night,» «darkness» to embody the negative suggestions: old age, decadence, solitude, oblivion, death; and on the opposite symbols of «light,» «sun,» «clarity» to state affirmation: life, youth, love. The poem «Cave of Night» is a good example because of the concentration of such symbolism; the central idea, which is generally the same as the others but stressing more the exaltation of the miracle of loving company, is defined through an anxious interplay of recurrent images of shadow and light which resolve into a nervous claroscuro:

> Look at it.   Here kissing you, I say it.   Look at it.
> In this dark cave, look, look at
> my kiss, my final darkness that covers with definitive
> night
> your luminous dawn
> that breaks
> in black, and like a sun within me announces to me
> another truth.   Which you, deep, ignore.
> From your being my clarity comes to me whole
> from you, my funeral dawn that opens into night.
> You, my nocturnity that, light, blinds me.

Thus in the awareness of existing as night or darkness, the loving *you* has entered zigzagging like light, reflecting against the background by means of sudden, rapid lexical brilliances which the sinuous and abrupt syntax expressively reinforces.

But it has also been pointed out that toward the center of the book the implacable statement of temporal reality comes close to hallucinatory glimpses. As a result, the poetic word is liberated from its general quality of sustained concentration; to a greater extent here, it makes use of irrational values or of the free association which they permit. Notice how, in the following quotation from «The One Who Was,» the image of integrated extinction of man and world which fatally culminates the whole process of creation is developed. Each one of the imaginative elements assembled here would permit a rational reduction. What is most surprising, on the whole, is the vast disquieting image of cosmic desolation that avoids vagueness because of Aleixandre's clarity; this clarity mixes phrases and expressions of literal meaning with the freest symbols and visions:

> *The diconnected moon has burned out*
> *on men.   The entire valley has died.*
> *The shadow invades its memory, and would be*
> *dust imagined, if it existed.   And not fantasy.*
> *Since mineral the earth has anticipated*
> *matter; man has aspired here.*
> *A gold devoured, a wind cold:*
> *that close breath is a cloud.*
> *It wants to last.   There is no stone.   Man loved.*

On these occasions, the poem becomes longer, the verse looser, the imagination freer, so that at times it seems to escape the logical imperative of the symbol.   But it would be hasty even to speak of surrealism or of how Aleixandre practised it with great originality.

What is really happening, as much in the overall trajectory of the book as in the passages of greatest expressive freedom, is that the author of *Poems of Consummation* simply returns to a realization that symbolism has been and still is the only unimpeded doorway to profound poetry.   Does this mean that *Poems of Consummation* is a symbolist or a neosymbolist book?   Not if that presupposes associating it with an abstract and dehumanized aesthetic. But we could relate it to symbolism if we mean to indicate that the author has pursued in this book what is inherent in symbolism: in-depth observation, the intention to know and reveal the most intimate and the ultimate certainties, the desire for total liberty. What we have discovered in *Poems of Consummation* is a tension between reality and human reality.   There is no superficial realism, no literal reproduction of circumstances, no clerical transcription of situations, nor any defense of implicit doctrines, extra-poetic and often sub-poetic modes cultivated by post war poets because of their historical imperative.

Recent Spanish poetry is today going against the limitations we have just mentioned.   Aleixandre has cautiously watched the changes which the dynamic nature of style has imposed;   he has also made clear his desire not to stay «entirely at the edge of the living current of poetry.»(5)   Thus, when Spanish poets accepted as norm the lyrical testimony of man's existence in his historical time, the author of *History of the Heart* accepted and assimilated this, avoiding the pitfalls of prosaicness and propagandism.   Now that poetry appears to be dedicating more care to the exploration of the unknown areas of human knowledge and to the improvement of the expressive quality of the verse, Aleixandre gives us the beautiful *Poems of Consummation* in which the terseness and brilliance of expression naturally accompany an authentic content based on lucid introspection.   Thus he takes his place in the living current of Spanish poetry which he himself has helped to form.

NOTES

1.   For more on the theme of utopia as the powerful motor agent of Aleixandre's most original poetic conceptions, see my essay «Vicente Aleixandre in Two Times,» in my book *Cinco poetas del tiempo,* second enlarged edition, Madrid: Insula, 1972.

2.   The poet himself has considered *Poems of Consummation* a «tragic book.» Consult «Prólogo y notas a *Mis poemas mejores*» contained in *Obras completas,* second edition, Madrid: Aguilar, 1977, II, 557.   On this same page, the author adds something that might cast light on our position: «And that which is inexorable in consummation is assumed as a knowledge which is in itself a value, I would say a dark illumination.»

3.   Aleixandre clarifies that in this book «he attempts to sing with grave voice and appropriate gesture the situation of the old man who lives the full awareness of youth as the equivalent of the only life.»   *Obras completas,* second edition, II, 557.

4.   The rational distinction between knowing (conocer) and known (saber) will be resolved in the following book *Dialogues of Knowledge*, in favor of a dark and nihilistic identification that will emerge as a substance symbolic of the impotence of any cognitive effort, and it will pose the need for silence as the only kind of final and supreme knowledge.

5.   *Obras completas*, second edition, II, 543.

«KNOWING» AND «KNOWN» IN
POEMS OF CONSUMMATION
AND *DIALOGUES OF KNOWLEDGE*

Guillermo Carnero
Universidad de Valencia

1. *An aleixandrine leitmotif and its tranformation*

The major premise of aleixandrine discourse is, as Carlos
Bousoño has indicated in his excellent book, vitality, at least in
what is considered the first stage of his poetic production which
comes to a close with the publication of *The History of the Heart.*
The vitality to which I refer is double: on the one hand it is the
act of recognition of the world which surrounds the poet, or rather
his intuition, since the word «recognition» is condemned in
Aleixandre's universe as is manifest in the texts which serve as the
subject of this study; on the other hand, it is evidence for the poet
of his own vitality.   In this way, existence in the world is, for
Aleixandre, a harmony which is felt and enjoyed and does not need
to be provoked because it is given between the being of the
individual and the being of reality: between these there is more
than communication (communication would presuppose the
existence, at least at the beginning, of two expressivities which
then turn out to be in agreement).   There is a unique expression,
which is the language of what is alive in the universe, of which the
poet is a part differentiated only insofar as he is endowed with
consciousness.   I would dare say that there is no communication,
because the relationship world-poet occurs at a level of greater
identity in which the poet does not feel alien: «I am that happy
earth that doesn't bargain for its reflection» («Ultimate Birth»).
The poet feels so full of life that, in a typical aleixandrine vision,
he grows until he touces the clouds and his extended arms take
in the four cardinal directions.

As Bousoño has noted, this first long stage is a continuing
canto to elemental beings, natural elements and animals, espe-

cially wild animals, including those which, like the beetle, wander
serenly through a benevolent universe.   In their massive, solid,
motionless existence, the inorganic elements manifest evidence
of life.   The animals manifest the preeminence of impulse and
instinct: Aleixandre calls «love» the energy of the tiger, endowed
with «a heart that knows almost nothing, except love» («The
Jungle and the Sea»).   As he states in «The Poet,» the vibrant
poet sees himself reflected in nature:

> *for you, poet, who felt in your breath*
> *the brutal charge of the celestial birds,*
> *and in whose words the powerful wings of eagles fly as fast*
> *as the back of the warm fishes flash without sound:*

After *History of the Heart*, the poet takes a step backwards;
still immersed in the vital plan of the world, he no longer keeps
step with it; he separates himself from things and, always ready
to jump back into the world, he considers them from a certain
distance in the two books which form the transitional stage in the
development of his work: *In a Vast Dominion* and *Portraits
with a Name*.   In these two books, the attitude of Aleixandre
could be summed up by what Bousoño has called «solidarity» to
explain the way the poet approaches the characters of his *Encounters.* By «solidarity,» I understand an attitude toward the world
which is becoming tinged with nostalgia; it is not sad because the
separation has been voluntary as well as recent: the poet does not
yet feel it as an imposition (in all that follows I am referring to the
two transitional works, not to the *Encounters*).   The intensity of the
relationship to the world diminishes and solidarity is another name
for inertia.   Separate from the poet, the characters in *Portraits
with a Name* provoke in him an enormous sympathy.   It is
especially the first chapter in *In a Vast Dominion* where Aleixandre's fervor for young bodies, for the flesh in all of its manifestations, for youth, sustains an obvious trace of nostalgia: an
inventory is made of a series of parts of the human body which
Aleixandre contemplates now not with his normal exaltation but
rather with amazement at its exact functioning and its perfect
mechanisms.   This is reminiscent of Leonardo's reflections on the
appropriateness of anatomical organization;   the enthusiasm
has become intellectual, mixed in with the memory the senses
bring to bear.   This reflective attitude is not yet tinged with
disillusion; but what the reading of *Poems of Consummation*

will reveal to us about this attitude is that, in the first chapter of *In a Vast Dominion*, the relationship between Aleixandre and the world is substantially modified.

In *In a Vast Dominion*, the poet's life pauses to be contemplated and acquires a clear meaning: it is the passage of time which contains moments of immersion into the universe. This immersion still seems possible, and the moment when the poet considers that his past is linked to the past itself there is no break in time because there is no separation from life; the poet thinks that he has simply made a stop on the way, and before resuming the journey, he looks back and takes comfort in it. As *Poems of Consummation* will show, this stop was not a pause, but rather a definitive stopping. «The Old Man Is like Moses» well sums up the key idea of this work. Like Moses, the poet sees before him a future life which others will enjoy.

With *Poems of Consummation*, a new element in Aleixandre's world bursts forth: old age. It is not surprising that it is charged with dark tones if we recall the emphasis on life and on love, the gifts of youth, in the first eight books. Age sets margins: «But the one who passes alone, protected/ by his age, crosses without being sensed» («The Years»); and in «Final Face» it turns the being into a grotesque caricature:

> *That is why, when the old man exhibits his hilarious*
> *vision he sees himself behind bars*
> *degraded, the recollection of some living, and there appears*
> *the pointed nose, eaten on gnawed away, the thinning hair,*
> *a mat, the turbid drop that makes up the eye, and the*
> *hollow or crack*
> *where the mouth was. . .*

Old age is the ongoingness of an incomplete existence, because living is loving and being loved: «The one who could have been was not. Nobody has loved him» («The One Who Was»). The world is, by virtue of love, «Lyre opened of the world» («The Young Lovers»). Life is linked to youth which is its indispensable requisite: «Life is being young and nothing more» («He Doesn't Know It»). «I was young and I looked, I burned,/ I touched, I sounded» («Sound of War»). And the lesson of age is a paradox: one can only hope for immortality, unaltered permanence in time which is the negation of life: only dead things remain as they are and this state is the only one invulnerable to time: «. . . the leaves reflected fall. They fall and they last. They live» («If Anyone Had Told Me»).

2. «*Knowing*» *and* «*known*»(1)

In *Poems of Consummation* it is stated clearly: «Knowing is not the same as to know» (first line of the poem «A Term». As one continues reading the book it becomes evident that the two terms have a meaning which is not usual: Aleixandre goes polishing the meaning throughout the book which, from this perspective, turns out to be its progressive materialization. We witness this process of definition through which the attitude of Aleixandre toward the world becomes determined by the op- position between «knowing» and «known.» Through the function of these two terms and their derivatives like «truth,» the poet balances his life and exposes a new kind of relationship with the world. Furthermore, he assumes a concrete attitude toward the problem of writing. I shall try to expose the semantic content of these two key words: once the content is determined, *Poems of Consummation* will reveal a concrete meaning. The book is written in an alogical manner (which is very different from methodical illogicalness), nevertheless it is logically formulable and analyzable. I believe that these two characteristics, alogicalness in the writing and receptivity to logical analysis, permit the recognition of a great work rather than a mystification.

We know that in all of Aleixandre's work, life has been identified with the capacity for feeling love. This love can be understood in two ways: an animal loves when it sets itself in motion impelled by its instincts to communicate with its fellows and with nature: eating, killing, reproducing are episodes of this love. Man adds one ingredient to animal nature: his awareness of sharing animal instinct and especially his need to formulate in some way the attraction he feels toward what sur- rounds him and also the nature of this environment. Then, in the human being, there exists a supplementary manifestation of love: the desire for knowing and for knowing oneself in ad- dition to knowing the other (*conocer*). For Aleixandre, love is, combined with sense perception and beginning with not-knowing, a need for knowing. In «Lazarillo and the Beggar,» Lazarillo says: «I love because I do not know,» (*saber*). Knowing is not exclusive

to man, since it occurs not only on a rational level, but also on an
irrational level. The feeling experience, although deprived of
awareness, brings knowing; therefore, the bull comes to know his
experience of the bullfight and of death: «That bull knows
although he may be dying» («The Maja and the Old Woman»).
Although it may be impossible for him to elevate his experience to
another level different from the level of feeling because of the
limitations of his nature and because the feeling experience
immediately precedes his death, he knows his experience. The
verb «knowing» has, in the alexandrine context, an uncompleted
value reinforced by the same value of the other verb which, in the
same context, is closely connected to it: the verb «looking.»
«Knowing» and «looking» embody the unfinished process, the
unsatisfied aspiration, the unfinished journey in the same way that
«to know» and «to see» indicate termination and completion.
«Looking» is the questioning and inquisitive attitude of the one
who seeks to apprehend a meaning of which he is still ignorant,
and «looking» is associated, in the aleixandrine text, with youth:
«the one who looked and who did not see. . . youth beating in his
hands» («But Born»); «Knowing, penetrating, inquiring: a
passion that lasts as long as life» («Darkness»); «the one who
gropes, lives» (Sound of War»). For this reason, «knowing,»
which is equivalent to being alive, is also equivalent to being
uncertain about what one is trying to know: in the poem «The
Young Lovers» (which I believe took its inspiration from the story
of Calixto and Melibea)(2), he says: «. . . I glimpsed her: I am
knowing her./ And this garden hides from me behind its walls
her form,/ not her radiance.» Love is born from a sudden vision,
from a «radiance,» and it impels one to apprehend the significance
of the beloved and in this apprehension is its climax because, with
the termination of the cognitive process, comes also the termination of the stimulus which attracts to the beloved: «Knowing is
loving. To know, to die/ I doubted. Never is love life» («The
Old Lovers»).

     And life lasts as long as the desire to apprehend the world
has not been satiated: «What insistence on living. I only understand it/ as *formulation* of the impossible: the real/ world»
(«The Old Lovers»; italics mine). Let us stress the word *formulation;* a formula is a condensation of meaning which we consider
definitive: a formula is the product of reason, and reason is
proper to the old because it produces its edicts when the cognitive

process has ended: «Only the child is knowing» (The Comet»);
«I am young and I am knowing» («The Young Lovers»).

When the cognitive process has ended, the one who under-
took the process now has a wisdom: knowing is an activiy, and to
know is a fixed result. Wisdom comes with age, and since old
age is incompatible with vitality, and wisdom is acquired after the
process of knowing has been completed, this wisdom is opposed to
life: «The one who doubts exists. Only dying is science»
(«Without Faith»); «Not knowing is living. To know, dying it»
(«Yesterday»).   I want to stress the transitive use of the verb
«dying.»   This «it» does not mean the biological life of the poet
but all that life means in Aleixandre's context; the transitive value
of «dying» shows that death is not a state but rather the result
of an activity.   Aleixandre means that he is not dealing with the
death of the body (that, in Spanish, would be the reflexive use of
the verb to die) but with the annihilation of something larger than
the body itself but so linked with its survival that the poet cannot
say «kill it.»   With «killing it,» he would also die; hence the great
suggestive power of the transitive «dying it.»

Wisdom is incompatible with youth and life as I have already
said: «Because I know it I do not exist» («You Have a Name»).

To know is to be born to science whose subject is the world
and, at the same time, it is the death of life. What Aleixandre
suggests is that he considers the evolution of the mind and of the
body irreconcilable: the body advances through time driven by
its senses and its desire for knowing and gradually it provides the
mind with facts and experiences from which the mind induces
wisdom. When the body stops functioning, the mind takes
account and draws up conclusions: there are no conclusions
until the acquisition of experience has ceased; these conclusions
(to know - known) demonstrate that immersion into life (knowing)
has stopped; the moment one «is born» (to the known), one «dies»:
«More young people see each other. They are the non-dead,/
since they are the non-born» («The Young»). Swan, in «That
Swan's Way,» says:

> ...I climbed the ladder
> of that knowing.   But I thought how useless
> it was to know it. . .

So once in possession of the known, the world loses its newness because each new experience becomes foreseeable and explain-able by virtue of the known: «looking» becomes equivalent to «seeing» and the effort of «knowing» a new reality becomes frustrated in the «re-cognition» that that reality is similar to a previous reality already codified by the known. To know, which seemed to be the optimal relationship with the world because of the desire for knowing in the one who loves, turns out to be, once achieved, a wall between the lover and the beloved, between man and the world, and the poet tells us that the only desirable knowing would be that which results from an unpremeditated relationship with the world in which no knowing whatsoever was sought, in which only living was sought. Then one would have extracted from the world a known not subject to formulation and not accompanied by the signs of dying: «. . . the one who doesn't look is knowing» («You Are Waiting»); «The light, once thought, deceives» («The Limit»). The desire for the known grew out of a mistaken idea: to consider that the world had to be ap-prehended in scientific terms, that sensorial contact was not sufficient, that it was necessary to name it and to formulate it, as expressed in «Present, Afterwards»:

> To place my lips on your idea is to feel you
> a proclamation.   Oh yes, terrible, you exist.
> I am the one who expired, the one who pronounced your name
> like form
> while I was dying.

Thus it turns out that to know is equivalent to being dead: «because I know I am falling asleep» («Lazarillo and the Beggar»); «the one who remembers is the one who is dying» («The Young Lovers»); here «to remember» is used with the meaning described above «to recognize»: «the one who knows has already lived» («The Old Lovers»). True wisdom would be, as I have previously stated, having «known» how to maintain an unpremeditated relationship with the world, relating to it in a perpetual knowing which can never be considered definitive, like the Rubén Darío Aleixandre sketched in «Knowing Rubén Darío.» This wise man, always wandering and always alive, would be one of the «creatures of the dawn» of whom Aleixandre speaks in *Shadow of Paradise*: «You encountered the generous light of innocence» (first line of «Creatures in the Dawn»), «naked with majesty and purity facing

the world's scream» («Message»; this does not mean «deprived
of majesty and purity,» by invested with them by virtue of nakedness); «. . . being in the movement with which the great heart of
men beats extended» («In the Plaza»).

We can, then, establish two series of analogous terms through
which the recent Aleixandre expresses himself and orders his
vision of the world: on the one hand, knowing--youth--life--
looking--experience of the senses; on the other hand, known--old
age--death--seeing--the conclusions of thought. If one under-
takes to read *Poems of Consummation* and *Dialogues of Knowledge* taking these two master series into account, their deepest
meaning emerges.(3)

One could also establish that «light» and «air,» used
metaphorically, are associated with «knowing,» while «sound»(4)
is associated with «known.» The explanation could be that knowledge is formulated in words and words are articulated sounds.
But I would rather pass over these associations which might not
be valid, considering the very general value of natural elements
in Aleixandre's poetry.

If wisdom is formulated in words, then Aleixandre has
articulated the problems of expression and of writing and
examined them with an essentially disenchanted view. Words
are not always signs of death; they aren't when they rise
spontaneously as a manifestation of vitality, as can be seen in
«The Words of the Poet»:

> . . . *words spoken*
> *in moments of delight or anger, of ecstasy or abandon,*
> *when, the soul awakened looms in the eyes*

In other situations, which are in fact the majority, words have a
sterilizing quality, as in «Sound of War»:

> . . . *(they) are merely words*
> *that drag you, a dust shadow,*
> *smoke exploded, human as you turn out*
> *like an idea dead beyond nothingness.*

Already in *Swords like Lips,* Aleixandre had established the antithetical nature of words and elemental beings. In «Words,»
he writes:

> *Flower you, girl almost naked, alive, alive*
> *(the word, that mashed sand).*
> ....
> *(The word, the word, the word, what a clumsy swollen womb).*

In «Message,» from *Shadow of Paradise*, we read: «. . .without looking, cast far away the sad articles,/ sad clothes, words, blind stakes.» The living word is characterized by being a non-definitive formulation, an attempt to formulate; overly expert expression is symptomatic that one has reached the stadium of wisdom. As is seen in «The Words of the Poet,» living words are ordered according to their own logic:

> *more like light than like expert sound.*
> ....
> *... Not with supreme virtue,*
> *but yes with an order, infallible, if they want.*

The wise man's desire is that his expert words recover the tremor and the fallibility they had when they were alive. Because wisdom as Aleixandre understands it, provides a kind of truth which the poet rejects after having sought it: only the incomplete and imperfect truth of knowing has value and radiates light and life: «. . . if it goes out, it is dead» («The Maja and the Old Woman»).

NOTES

1. In translating this article and the poems cited in it, I have consistently stated the distinction *conocer*, «knowing,» and *saber* «to know» or «known.» English does not differentiate these two «knowings» nor does it accomodate related words, such as: *conocimiento*, «knowledge,» *sabiduría*, «wisdom,» *ignorar*, «not to know,» *reconocer*, «to recognize,» *reconocimiento*, «recognition.» As Carnero

says, the subtle distinctions in Aleixandre's poetry have been elaborated gradually, consequently it has been impossible to be consistent in the translation of these terms throughout the poems; it is a particular problem with the poems in *Dialogues of Knowledge.* For the English-speaking reader, John Dewey and Arthur F. Bentley, in *Knowing and the Known* (Boston: Beacon Press, 1949), clarify many of the problem terms relating to this article and to Aleixandre's poetry, which stem from the problem of language itself. Dewey and Bentley state: «Knowings are always and everywhere inseparable from the knowns--the two are twin aspects of common fact (p. 53).» Later: «Knowings: Organic phases of transactionally observed behaviors (pp. 296-297.» In *Dialogues of Knowledge,* Aleixandre elaborated a poetic epistemology in dialogue; throughout his work, he has sought to create a poetic universe that is to be apprehended in itself: by knowing.

2.   This is a reference to the young lovers in the Spanish masterpiece *La Celestina* (1499), which has been widely translated into English.

3.   *Conocer* and *saber* also have, besides the meaning described here, an extended usage in which the terms retain their proper sense at the same time that they incorporate the sense of the other term.   For example «Loving is knowing (*conocer*).   The one who lives knows (*saber*).»   («Knowing Rubén Darío»).   «The one who lives, gropes.   The one who is knowing (*conocer*) has died» («Sound of War»), and «Be quiet, you do not know (*conocer*)» («The Maja and the Old Woman»). These special cases do not invalidate the normal aleixandrine definition of the two terms.

4.   In translating, it was impossible to represent the two Spanish words for sound-- *son,* a general abstract term, and *sonido* a more particular reference.

TRANSLATOR'S NOTE

A year ago I set out to translate into English the articles in this book in order to share their critical insights with the reader interested in Aleixandre's poetry who might be unfamiliar with Spanish criticism or with Spanish.* As I worked on the articles, I began looking for existing translations of the poetry to use in the texts. Two things immediately became apparent: very few of Aleixandre's poems are available to the English reader (and very little information about the poet), and the few translations that do exist were so distant from the original that they did not fit with the analyses. Hence it became necessary to supply English versions of the poems analyzed in the studies, versions meticulously close in language, structure, tone and meaning.

In the summer of 1978, after translating and digesting the content of the articles, I began to translate, in its entirety, each poem which is quoted extensively in the texts (citations of three or more lines, which appear indented, totaling fifty-five in all; because of length, the prose poems are not included). The criteria which guided my work are three-fold, listed in order of priority: 1) to be as true to the original as the two languages permit; 2) to be true to the critical appreciations; and 3) to present English renditions which are meaningful and artistic in their own right.

In turning the Spanish to English, I sought always to maintain word equivalence, comparable structure and identical punctuation. On very few occasions, it was necessary to rearrange the elements between two lines of verse, and this mostly because of adjective placement. One of the persistent difficulties of translating from Spanish to English is, in fact, adjective usage, and this problem is complicated in Aleixandre's poetry by his cultivation of ambiguous reference and juxtaposition. Spanish adjective agreement according to number and gender permits a greater flexibility in word placement and suggests other and more varied relationships than are possible in English. An example of this complexity occurs in «The Old Lovers,» where the word «dura» is used on three occasions. Because the theme of the poem is time, I have rendered this word «it lasts,» but it simultaneously means «hard.» The second line typifies this ambiguity: «The afternoon is beautiful, and it lasts» or «The afternoon is beautiful, and hard» («La tarde es bella, y dura»). Besides the triple occurrence of this pun, there are various other examples of word-play and echoes referring to this word, such as «duda,» «muda» and «durable.» These nuances are lost in the translation.

Aleixandre relies on apparently simple colloquial expression in his verse, and it is precisely the everyday expressions that introduce ambiguity and uncertainty into the poems. Examples from the same poem are repetitions of «the one who» and patterns like «Existing is shining» («Existir es brillar») or «Being is not loving» («Ser no es amar»). In Spanish, the infinitive suggests two different states: the capacity, the power «to love,» and also the infinite process of «loving.» (This distinction was a significant difficulty in the translation of Carnero's «Knowing and *Known* in *Poems of Consummation*» which was compounded by the different vocabulary items).

Similarly, the Spanish gerund form has different connotative values: its use implies «cause-because» and also the affirmation of being itself: «by virtue of-being.» The following two lines exemplify this complexity: «Yo no dudo. Yo canto. Hermosa he sido;/ soy, digo, pues lo fui. Lo soy, pues, siéndolo.» To explain, this means: I do not doubt. I sing. I have been beautiful; I am, I mean, since I was it (beautiful). I am it (beautiful), then, being it (beautiful). «Being it» suggests that she was and is beautiful because and by virtue of being beautiful. Beauty causes beauty because it is beauty. This demonstrates that in Aleixandre's poetry, ordinary language usage becomes laden with meaning because of his constant effort to redefine the edge of knowing, the edge of being, the edge of relationship.

Another example of ambiguity occurs in his use of pronouns, complicated in Spanish by the ability to omit the subject pronoun. Thus Spanish pronoun usage, including the omission of the subject pronoun, presents an unspecified and often multiple reference which is normally impermissible in English. Consequently at times, I had to restrict the sense by referring to a more specific antecedent than suggested in the original. Furthermore, this process of specification takes place naturally in English because of a more fixed word order and logic.   To exemplify this kind of ambiguity, I cite the first part of «The Old Lovers»: «Oye la tierra/ cómo gime larga.   Son sus pasos, o su idea.» («Hear the earth/ how it moans long.   They are steps, or their idea»).   In this instance, the verb «oye» can mean, as translated, «hear,» a command.   Its other potential subjects are: «the earth hears,» or it can refer back to the previous statement «the afternoon hears» or it can refer to an unspecified «he,» «she,» «you,» «it» hears.   That is, there are seven potential subjects for this verb. The following verb «gime,» «moans,» is likewise ambiguous.   In this citation, the subject of «son» is entirely nonspecific; I have used the vague «they» in English which, like the Spanish, has no clear antecedent, although grammatically «steps» functions as the subject.   More difficult is the meaning of the possessive «su,» which can refer to: his, her, your, its, their, to any third person possessor.   We cannot be sure, nor, in my opinion, should we be sure, *whose* idea it is.   The English «their» which I chose to use is restrictive because it seems to refer specifically to «steps.»

This conscious exploitation of ambiguity creates a density in Aleixandre's poetry because of the way in which disparate elements are joined together.   This process of unification and of accumulated layering of experience on experience within one poem and within his total production has been difficult to communicate in English because of our tendency to fix and to focus on the logical specific referent.   Spanish adjectives which show number and gender, and pronoun usage which can suggest a larger frame of reference, represent two kinds of expression cultivated by Aleixandre to create his poetic universe which do not transfer readily into English.

At the same time that there is this kind of unification through ambiguous reference, there is also (as these articles stress), an almost shocking contradiction and apparent disjunction in Aleixandre's poetry.   I have made a conscious effort to preserve this strain and tension since, in my opinion, it is the heart of his creative power (in this connection, incidentally, Aleixandre would use the word «entrañas,» «vital organs,» «guts,» «cescera,» «inwards» which was one of the most challenging words to render in English).   In revising my translations, I noticed that the later modifications produced a rougher, more jarring English than the first versions.   This clashing is deliberate, since it is intended to capture the latent violence and also the rhythms of the original. It is also intended to encourage the reader to read the poem aloud. Aleixandre's vision must be heard. It must be heard not only because of the value of the sounds and the effect of the unusual ordering of elements, but especially in order to recreate the whole, to bring it into existence in a spacio-temporal context. To experience this effect, I recommend reading aloud «The Poet Sings for Everyone,» which ends «And a sky of a power, completely existent,/ now with majesty makes the whole echo of man.» Each word, even in English, possesses its complex being, which transmits to the reader a sense of how Aleixandre re-orders thinking, feeling, being, language. The single word I would use to describe this process is «transubstantiation.»

To conclude these remarks about my translations, I refer the reader to the poems in their original language, which is neither normally difficult in itself nor inaccessible to the person who has studied several years of Spanish. By using these translations as a means to enter the world of Aleixandre's creation, the reader will discover a universe of beauty and meaning not always evident in my translations, the realm of relating, knowing, loving.

I take this opportunity to thank the authors of the critical studies for their suggestions concerning my translations of their work and especially to thank my good friend and colleague Vicente who worked closely with me to render these poems as «true» as possible.

Harriet Boyer

NOTE

*   «A literary Generation and a poet» by Vicente Cabrera and «The 'Isakower' Phenomenon and the Dream Screen» by Kessel Schwartz were originally written in English.

POEMS IN TRANSLATION

ULTIMATE BIRTH

To end, this alert attitude.
Alert, alert, alert.
I am awake or beautiful.   I am the sun or the answer.
I am that happy earth that doesn't bargain for its reflection.
When the day is born a town cry or jubilations are heard.
Senseless the abyss has insisted all night long.
But this happy company of the air,
this illumination of recollections that has become illuminated like an atmosphere,
has let the least creatures breathe,
molecules themselves turned into light or into traces of footsteps.
To my step I have sung because I have dominated the horizon;
because above it--further, further still, because I am very tall--
I have seen the sea, the sea, the seas, the non-limits.
I am tall like youth which doesn't cease.
Where is that head going to reach that has already broken three thousand windowpanes,
those countles roofs that forget that they were flesh in order to turn into deafness?
Toward what skies or what ground go those untrodden eyes
that have as a yolk an invisible fecundity?
Toward what mourning or disorders do those abandoned hands plunge down
blindly?

What clouds or what palms, what kisses or perennials
seek that forehead, those eyes, that dream,
that growth that will end like a newborn death?

AT THE BOTTOM OF THE WELL (THE BURIED MAN)

There at the bottom of the well where the little flowers,
where the lovely daisies do not wave,
where there is no wind or perfume of man,
where never the sea imposes its threat,
there, there that silence is quiet
like a noise choked by a fist.

If a bee, if a flying bird,
if that error which is never expected
happens,
the cold remains;
vertical sleep plunged the earth down
and already the air is free.

Perhaps a voice, a hand already loosed,
an impulse upwards aspires to the moon,
to calm, to warmth, to that poison
of a pillow over a choking mouth.

But sleeping is always so serene!
On the cold, on the ice, on a cheek's shadow,
on a lifeless word, and, now gone,
on the earth itself always virgin.

A board at the bottom, oh unnumbered well,
that illustrious smoothness that proves
that a back is contact, it is dry cold,
it is always sleep even if the forehead is closed.

Clouds can pass now.   Nobody knows.
That clamor. . .   Do the bells exist?
I recall that the color white or the forms,
I recall that the lips, yes, even they were speaking.

It was the hot time.   --Light, immolate me--.
It was then when the lightening suddenly
hung suspended like iron.
Time of sighs or of «worship me,»
when the birds were never losing feathers.

Time of softness and permanence;
the galloping wasn't in the breast,
the hoofbeats didn't stay, they were not wax.
Tears were rolling down like kisses.
And in the ear the echo was not solid.

Thus eternity was the minute.
Time alone a tremendous hand
on the long hair detained.

Oh yes, in this deep silence or humidity,
beneath the seven layers of blue sky I do not know
the music congealed into sudden ice,
the throat that collapses over the eyes,
the intimate wave which floods the lips.

Asleep like fabric
I feel the grass grow, the smooth green
that is uselessly waiting to be curved.

A steel hand on the grass,
a heart, a forgotten toy,
a spring, a file, a kiss, a windowpane.

A metal flower thus impassive
sucks from the earth a silence or memory.

THE MOST BEAUTIFUL LOVE

Distant day before yesterday.
One very remote day
I ran into the windowpane never seen,
with a butterfly tongue,
with that vibration escaped from where it had been held.

I had cried for ten centuries
like ten drops fused
and I had felt myself with the beauty of the unhappened
contemplating the velocity of the express.

But I comprehended that everything was false.
False the form of the cow that dreams
of being a lovely budding maiden.
False the affair of the false professor who has hoped
in the end to comprehend his nakedness.
False even the simple way girls
at night hang up their untouched breasts.

But I found myself a shark in the form of affection;
no, no; in the form of a well loved shark;
clean squalus, extendible heart, burning or crime,
delicious possession that consists of the sea.
Tormented clouds in the end turned into cheeks,
storms like blue over the one seeking exhaustion,
sweet viscous embrace of the largest and the blackest,
that imperious form that tastes like infinite slippery.

Thus, without ending mutely that bloody coupling,
breathing in above all a thick ink,
kisses are stains, extendible stains
that the most delicate hands cannot tear from me.

A mouth imposing like a bestial fruit,
like a dagger that threatens love from the sand,
a bite that might take   in all the water or night,
a name that resounds like a rolling roar,
everything whispered by lips I adore.

Tell me, tell me the secret of your anticipated sweetness,
of that skin that reserves its truth systolically;
sleep in my arms like a conquered nut,
like a minimal being that forgets its cataclisms.

You are a point alone, a comma or eyelash;
you are the greatest monster of the unique ocean,
you are that mountain that by navigating occupies
the bottom of the seas like an overflowing heart.

I penetrate you silently while I scream or rip,
while my howling makes music or sleep,
because I kiss walls, walls which will never have eyes,
and I kiss that easy yolk as sensitive as the feather.

The truth, the truth, the truth is what I say,
that immense pistol that lies in the road,
that silence--that very one--that finally stays
when with a first broom I brush aside the paths.

WORDS

But it doesn't matter that everything is calm.
(The word, that withered wool).
Flower you, girl almost naked, alive, alive
(The word, that mashed sand).
Girl, with your shadow what a sweet struggle
like a fleeting honey that almost has edges.
(The word, the word, the word, what a clumsy, swollen womb).
Girl, you are stained with delicate foam.

Paper.   Tongue of mourning.   Threat.   Putrefaction.
Words, words, words, words.
Wrath, Bestial.   Clumsiness.   Yellowness.
Words against wind or thighs, dirty.

Don't wait for me, clever, weak ship,
weak turned face that passes
over a sea of nacre held up by hands.
Ship, paper or mourning, edge or womb,
word that gets lost like sand.

SALON

A paper bird
and an incarnate feather,
and a fury of silk,
and a white dove.

A whole bouquet of myrtle
or of colored shadows,
a pulsing marble
and a love that advances.

An obsequious swaying
of moments or pauses,
a salon of valkyries
or of fainting ladies.

A music or nard
or some spiderwebs,
a jug of exhaustion
and of powders or mother-of-pearl. . .

Everything sweet and pained,
everything of white flesh;
yellowness and circles under the eyes,
and wick and estate.

Love, turns, falls,
butterflies, glances,
smiles like wires,
where wax sings:
birds, box, music,
sleeves, flights and dance,
with breasts sounding
under the pale flames.

Waists or saliva,
threads of fine silver,
kisses for the golden
lemons that were hanging.

you wear bellies or shells
who bump into tin flesh,
you place kisses or lichens
for low humidities,

You wear bellies or shells
or lazy boats
and armpits like roses
loosed in the early morning,

mysteries of cheeks
loved adrift
and ears and hair,
fainting spells, low voices. . .

Wide gulf detained
by the low bank,
salon of moss and moon
where love is algae,
where damp clothing
is skin which doesn't rip off
when between polka and breeze
the lank dawn breaks.

UNITY IN HER

Happy body that flows in my hands,
face well-loved in which I contemplate the world,
in which graceful birds are copied fugitives
flying to the region where nothing is forgotten.

Your external form, diamond or hard ruby,
brilliance of a sun that dazzles in my hands,
crater that invites me with its intimate music,
with that mysterious call of your teeth.

I die because I plunge, because I want to die,
because I want to live in the fire, because this air outside
is not mine, but rather the warm breath
which if I draw near burns and gilds my lips from a depth.

Let me, let me look, tinged with love,
face reddened by your crimson life,
let me look at the deep clamor of your inwards
where I die and renounce living forever.

I want love or death, I want to die entirely,
I want to be you, your blood, that raging lava
that enclosed by nourishing beautiful extremities
feels thus the beautiful limits of life.

This kiss on your lips like a slow thorn,
like a sea that flew off as a mirror,
like the flash of a wing,
is still hands, a touch of your crackling hair,
a crackling of the vengeful light,
light or mortal sword which over my throat is threatening,
but which will never be able to destroy the unity of this world.

THE LIGHT SEA

The sea punishes the clamor of dry boots
that pass without fear of treading on faces,
on those who kissing on the smooth sand
take on the forms of shells shut two by two.

The sea beats alone like a mirror,
like an illusion of air,
that vertical glass where the desert dryness
feigns water or sound of swords pursuing each other.

The sea, enclosed in a die,
unleashes its fury or prisoner drop,
heart whose borders whould flood the world
and can only contract with its smile or limit.

The sea pulses like a bird,
like that ability to fly to the skies,
aerial lightness of that which sustains nothing,
of that which is only a sigh of a youthful breast.

The sea or enamored feather,
or liberated feather,
or graceful slip,
the sea or fleeing foot
that cancels the abyss by fleeing with light body.

The sea or fresh palms,
palms that with pleasure give in the hands of virgins,
palms that repose in breasts having forgotten the deep,
delicious surface that a soft wind curls.

The sea perhaps or now the hair,
the adornment,
the ultimate crest,
the flower that nods in a bluish ribbon,
of the one that, if detached, will fly like pollen.

COME ALWAYS, COME

Don't draw near. Your forehead, your burning forehead, your inflamed
                                                                      forhead,
the traces of some kisses,
that brilliance which even by day is felt if you draw near,
that contagious brilliance that sticks in my hands,
that luminous river into which I sink my arms,
where I almost don't care to drink, for fear afterwards of an already
hard life of a star.

I don't want you to live in me the way light lives,
with that starry isolation that joins with its light,
whom love denies across the space
hard and blue that separates and doesn't join,
where each inaccessible star
is a solitude, moaning, that emits its sadness.

Solitude gleams in a world without love.
Life is a vivid cortex,
a rough motionless skin
where man cannot find his rest,
no matter how he applies his dream against a burnt out star.

But don't you draw near.   Your gleaming forehead, inflamed coal that
                                   tears from me my own consciousness,
refulgent duel in which I suddenly feel the temptation to die,
to burn my lips with your indelible touch,
to feel my flesh come undone against your burning diamond.

Don't draw near, because your kiss is prolonged like the impossible
                                   collision of the stars,
like space which suddenly takes fire,
propagating ether where the destruction of worlds
is a single heart that totally burns up.

Come, come, come like the dark extinct coal that contains a death;
come like the blind night that brings her face near me;
come like two lips marked with red,
with that long line that fuses metals.

Come, come, my love; come hermetic forehead, roundness almost rolling
that you show like an orbit that's going to die in my arms;
come like two eyes or two deep solitudes,
two imperious flames of a depth I don't know.

Come, come, death, love; come quickly, I destroy you;
come, for I want to kill or to love or to die or to give you everything;
come, for you roll like a fickle stone,
confused like a moon that asks me for my rays!

THE LIGHT

The sea, the earth, the sky, the fire, the wind,
the permanent world we live in,
the most remote stars that almost beg us,
that at times are almost a hand that caresses the eyes.

That arrival of light that rests on the forehead.
Where do you come from, where are you from, loving form which I feel breathe,
which I feel like a breast that would contain a music,
which I feel like the sound of celestial harps,
now almost crystalline like the sound of worlds?

Where are you from, celestial tunic with the form of the luminous ray
who caresses a forehead that lives and suffers, that loves like the living?
where from, you who as suddenly resemble the memory of a burning fire like
                                                    the iron that brands
as you soften on the tired existence of a head that comprehends you.

Your touch without moaning, your smiling arrival like lips from above,
the murmur of your secret in the ear that awaits,
wounds or brings dreams like the pronunciation of a name
that lips that shine alone can utter.

Contemplating right now these tender little animals that circle around
                                                    the earth,
bathed by your presence or silent scale,
revealed to their existence, guarded by muteness
in which only the beating of their blood is heard.

Looking at this our own skin, our visible body
because you reveal it, light who sends you I do not know,
light who comes still as if uttered by lips,
with the form of teeth or of a begged-for kiss,
with the heat still of a skin that loves us.

Tell me, tell me who it is, who calls me, who utters me, who clamors,
tell me what is this very remote send-off that begs,
what crying I hear at times when you are only a tear.
Oh you, trembling celestial light or desire,
fervent hope of a breast that isn't extinguished,
of a breast that laments like two long arms
capable of encircling a waist on earth.

Oh loving cadence of remote worlds,
of lovers who never utter their suffering,
of bodies that exist, of souls that exist,
of infinite skies that reach us with their silence!

SONG OF A DEATH GIRL

Tell me, tell me the secret of your virgin heart,
tell me the secret of your body under the earth,
I want to know why you are now water,
those fresh banks where naked feet bathe in foam.

Tell me why on your loose hair,
on your sweet grass caressed,
there falls, slips, caresses and goes away
a sun burning or reposed that touches you
like a wind that carries only a bird or a hand.

Tell me why your heart like a tiny jungle
waits under the earth for impossible birds,
that total song that above the eyes
dreams make when they go by without sound.

Oh you, a song to a body dead or living,
to a beautiful being that sleeps under the soil,
you sing stone colored, kiss or lip colored,
you sing as if the nacre were sleeping or breathing.

That waist, that weak volume of a sad breast,
that voluble curl that does not know the wind,
those eyes where silence floats alone,
those teeth which are of protected ivory,
that air that does not move any leaves not green . . .

Oh you, laughing sky who goes by like a cloud;
oh happy bird who laughs over a shoulder;
fountain, fresh flow who entangles the moon;
soft grass trodden by adored feet!

I AM THE DESTINY

Yes, I have loved you as never.

Why kiss your lips, if I know that death is near,
if I know that loving is only forgetting life,
closing one's eyes to the present darkness
in order to open them to the radiant limits of a body?

I won't read in books a truth that little by little rises like water,
I refuse that mirror which everywhere the mountains offer,
bare rock where my forehead is reflected
crossed by birds whose sense I do not know.

I won't peer into the rivers where the fish red with the flush of living,
attack the banks limits of their desire,
rivers from which ineffable voices arise,
signs I don't comprehend lying among the reeds.

I won't, no; I refuse to swallow that dust, that suffering earth, that
                                                                    bitten sand,
that security of living with which the flesh takes communion
when it comprehends that the world and this body
roll like that sign that the celestial eye doesn't understand.

I won't, no, clamor, raise the tongue,
project it like that stone that shatters up high,
that breaks the windows of those immense skies
behind which no one listens to the sound of life.

I will live, live like the hard grass,
like the wind or the snow, like the vigilant coal,
like the future of a child still unborn,
like the contact of lovers when the moon doesn't know them.

I am the music that under so much hair,
the world makes in its mysterious flight,
bird of innocence which with blood on its wings
goes to die on an oppressed breast.

I am the destiny that summons all those who love,
sole sea to which all radiating lovers will come
who seek their center, curled by the circle
that whirls like the rose resounding and total.

I am the horse that inflames its mane against the bare wind,
I am the lion tortured by his own mane,
the gazelle that fears the indifferent river,
the conquering tiger that lays waste the jungle,
the tiny beetle that also shines in the day.

No one can ignore the presence of the one who lives,
of the one who standing amidst the screaming arrows,
shows his transparent breast that doesn't prevent looking,
that will never be crystal in spite of its clarity,
because if you draw your hands near, you can feel the blood.

SEA ON EARTH

No, do not clamor for that hurried joy
that is latent when the dark music doesn't modulate,
when the dark spurt passes mysterious
like a river that scorns the landscape.

Happiness doesn't consist of squeezing hands
while the world hesitates on its axis,
while the moon turned into paper
feels that a wind by smiling curls it.

Perhaps the clamorous sea that might try one night to fit into a shoe,
the infinite sea that tried to be dew,
that sought to rest on a sleeping flower,
that tried to dawn like the fresh tear.

The resonant sea turned into a lance
lies on the dryness like a fish that's drowning,
it clamors for that water that can be the kiss,
that can be a breast to be torn and inundated.

But the dry moon doesn't respond to the reflection of the pale scales.
Death is a contraction of a glassy pupil,
it is that impossibility of waving the arms,
of raising a scream until it strikes a sky.

Death is silence in the midst of dust, in the midst of memory,
it is to wave terribly a tongue not of man,
it is to feel that salt congeals in the veins
coldly like a whitest tree in a fish.

Then joy, the dark joy of dying,
of comprehending that the world is a grain that will come apart,
the one that was born for a divine water,
for that immense sea that lies over the dust.

Joy will consist of coming apart like the miniscule,
of turning into the severe fishbone,
remains of an ocean that like the light went away,
drop of sand that was a giant breast
and that having left the throat like weeping lies here.

FORM WITHOUT LOVE

Enough, sadness, enough, enough, enough.

Think no more of those eyes that hurt you,
of that pure forehead closed within its walls,
of that blond hair, which one night waved.

One night!   One life,   a whole grief, a whole love, a whole sweet blood.
A whole light which I drank in from some veins,
in the middle of the night, and on radiant days.

I loved you . . . I don't know.   I don't know what love is.
I suffered you gloriously like blood itself,
like the painful hammer which gives life and kills.

I felt daily that life is death.
I knew what it is to love because I died every day.

But I never died.   One does not die.   One dies. . .
One dies on an emptiness, on an unloving shoulder.
On an earth indifferent to the very kiss.

You were so tender; you were there, remoteley, a long time ago,
you were as sweet as the wind in the leaves,
like a mound of roses for fixed lips.

Afterwards a vengeful flash, some enigmatic destiny,
some cursed light from a stormy sky,
with its purple lightning struck your pure forehead,
your sweet eyes,
those early lips.

And your phosphorous eyes shone without hope,
they shone upon a barren mountain without love,
and they burned forever without dawn,
a sky as low as hatred to cover me.

Who are you?   What face is that, what diamond hardness?
What marble reddened by the storm
unappeased by kisses, or by sweet memory?
I kiss your form, stone rose without blood.
Your breast silent where water slides down.
Your face where blue light never shines,
that pure path of bland glances.
I kiss your hands that do not fly to lips.
I kiss the dripping of a saddened sky.

But perhaps I kiss only my pure tears.

This stone I embrace as one embraces a bird,
an immense feathered bird in which to bury a face,
is not a bird, it is a rock, it is the hard mountain,
human body without life from whom I ask death.

BIRDS WITHOUT DESCENT

A blond hair waves.
Remote beaches can be seen, happy clouds, a wind so golden
that it would connect bodies on the pure sand.
Birds without descent flee through the blue.
They are almost desires, they are almost foam.
They are the leaves of a sky radiant with beaty,
where a thousand throats sing light without death.

A man sees, witnesses.   A man lives, sleeps.
A form breathes the way the sea shakes.
A breast waves always almost blue to its beaches.

No, don't confuse the sea, the inert sea, with an agitated heart.
Don't ever mix blood with such free foam.
The white color is wing, is water, is cloud, is sail;
but it is never a face.
But it is never, never, a pulsing of blood,
a delicate warmth which runs through a body.

That is why,
stretched out her, on the beach.
Stretched out there afterwards on the hard road.
Stretched out beyond, on the enormous mountain,
a man is unaware of the kind green of the seas,
he is unaware of its melodious and empty surf
and he does not know the eternal cannon of its foam.

On the earth it lies like pure grass.
A hurricane combs it the way it combs great oaks.
Its arms do not witness the arrival of the birds.
Birds without descent are white under the sky.

UNDER THE EARTH

No.   No.   Never.   Ever.
My heart does not exist.
It would be useless for you, one by one, like naked trees,
to pass by when the earth turns.
Useless for the light to sound in the leaves like a well loved wind
and sweetly imitate a calling heart.

No. I am the dark shadow which, among the roots of the trees
coils like a serpent making music.
A serpent thick like a tree trunk
under earth breathes without imagining the grass.

I know that a sky exists.   Perhaps a God who dreams.
I know that that radiant blue you wear in your eyes
is a small sky with a sleeping gold.

Under earth one lives.   The moisture is blood.
There are worms as small as unborn children.
There are tubers which inside grow like flowers.
They do not know that up above and free their petals
are pink, yellow, carmin or innocent.

There are stones that will never be eyes.   There are grasses that are sad saliva.
There are teeth in the earth that in the middle of dreams
move and chew what is never kiss.

Beneath the earth there exists, deeper, the rock,
the naked, the purest rock where only human beings could live,
where warmth is possible for naked flesh
which placed there would be splendid limpid flowers.

There is water under the earth.   Dark water, you know?
Water without sky.
Water which for millenia mutely awaits the face,
the pure or crystalline face to be reflected,
or that bird feather that tears an open sky.

Deeper, deeper, fire purifies.
It is the deserted fire where no one ever descends.
Exile forbidden to souls, to shades.
Vital organs which burn from solitude without numen.

You, you who live in the world,
are not the ones who pass by or who sleep in white chains,
toe ones who fly perhaps with the name of setting
or dawning or zenith,
you are not the ones who will know the destiny of a man.

IN A CEMETERY

Who calls me?   What tomb still half-open
sends me arms, vistas, fugitive glimpses
of a glance still exiting under the heavy stone?

Who among all the graves calls out to me?
I go under slow crying trees
to a woman in black in the rain.

I go under purple lights that seek
a breast, only a breast, never a breast.
I hear the distant sea, and among its nacres
I perceive the hollow nacre which still sings it.

There are other woods whose treetops turn
without music, kind to their sky.
I feel all of the graves half-open
and a chorus of glances overcomes me.

I still live, yes.   I still live and seek earth,
earth in my arms, while all the air
is filled with its dark birds,
while the silent black wings,
without feathers, encircle stone, blood,
seek my eyes where never will there be
tears for the thirst which is not quenched.

I hear in my heart another noble sea,
another sad thicket.   Another rain without water.
Another chorus of nacres and birds
who pursue a man among the stones.

HUMAN BURNING

Calm ship which floats along a river,
At times I wonder if your body is a bird.
At times if it is water, water or the river itself;
but always I embrace you like a voice between lips.

To kiss you is to pronounce you, oh joy, oh sweet fire uttered.
To kiss you is to pronounce you like a heat which would spurt from the breast,
....

But you, so beautiful, have blue eyes,
you have lashes where birds fly,
where a song tangles among feathers or wings
that turn the dawn blue when night fades.

Oh beautiful, beautiful!   I saw you, I saw you pass by snatching at the
                                                                constant reality,
naked like the burning stone,
soft like the voice of flowers when they are touched,
yellow in the day without a sun that did not dare.

Your lips are that smooth sadness that blinds when someone proffers his poor
                                                                human mouth;
they were, not a word,
but their very dream,
their imperious command that punishes with a kiss.

Dying is not that name that passed by as a child,
passed by noiseless like a fairy in mourning.
It is not that dark night, when the wolf licked
the hand, yellow, that is an offshoot in the fire.

Dying is not that very black hair that waves,
that shadowy blue that lies in a rock.
That fatal gleam where the moon clashes
and leaps like steel spit forth by other steel.

Dying, dying is having in one's arms a body
from which one can never escape as a man.
But perhaps staying like a drop of lead,
a visible remnant on earth of a supreme burning.

But you who rest here the way light rests on a summer afternoon,
you are proud like nakedness without trees,
violent like the reddened moon,
and burning like the river evaporated by a volcano.

But I caress you knowing that life withstands more than fire,
that some teeth kiss, kiss even without lips,
and that, beautiful or terrible, between eyelashes
enraged birds fly, and sing, or even call me

IT IS NO LONGER POSSIBLE

Do not say your name sending forth your music
like a lifeless fire overflowing,
like that moon which in winter spreads
its pensive dust over the bone.

Let the night squeeze the absence of the flesh,
the last nakedness anyone asks for;
let the moon roll through the stones of the sky
like an already dead arm without an inflamed rose.

A long time ago some light smelled like flowers.
But it doesn't smell like anything.
Don't say that death smells of nothing,
that love's absence smells of nothing,
that the absence of air, of shadow, smell of nothing.

The moon was dislodging then, there, remotely, a long time ago,
it was dislodging shadows and flooding with flashing roses
that region where a breast was beating.

But the moon is a bare bone with no accent.
It is not a voice, it is not a celestial cry.
It is its hard hollow, it is a wall where they resounded,
thick walls where the sound of kisses used to break.

A bone still wants to roll through a sky
of stone, wants to overcome its extinguished quiet.
It still wants to grip a rose of fire
and bring it close to lips of flesh to burn it.

TO LOVE

One day you came for men.
You were, perhaps, the sunrise.
But you were more the sea, the hard, terse, transparent, threatening sea
                                                                    seeking shores,
spitting up lights, leaving behind its fish without bones
and rolling across the feet of some human beings,
removed from the pain or the joy of a sky.

You came foaming, furious, sweet, warm, frozenly burning under the hard kisses
of a sun constant on burnt skin.

The forest fled, the trees flew off.
A shadow of birds darkened an intangible blue.
The rocks were covered with moss from a fable.
And there, remotely, invisible, the lions slept.

Delicate, tranquil, with eyes where light has never yet shone,
timeless eyes for normal living,
you came without shadow, without dress, without hatred,
smooth like the breeze linked with noon,
violent like doves who love,
cooing like those beasts unextinguished by a sunset,
shining in the day under an almost black sun.

No, you were not the river, the fleeing, the fore-sensed fleeing
                                                    of some colts toward the east.
Nor were you the terrible beauty of the forest.
I could not confuse you with the sound of wind over the grass,
where the face of a man hears the sweet earth.

Far off the cities were spreading their tentacular roots,
monsters of Nineveh, megatheres without shadow,
weighty constructions of a divinity sulphuriously overthrown,
who burns convulsing while the ground creaks.

But you came imitating the simple quiet of the mountain.
You came the way the warm feather falls from a shaken sky.
The way a rose grows in blind hands.
The way a bird spurts from an adored mouth.
Just like a heart beats against another breast.

The world, no one knows where it is, no one can decide about the truth
                                                                    of its light.

No one listens to its fast music, that is sings always covered
by the noise of a hidden blood.

No one, no one knows you, oh love, who arrive by a silent ladder,
by a road from another land invisible.
But I felt you, I saw you, I divined you.
You, mortal beauty who fought in my arms,
sea transitory, impetuous sea with wings as furious as kisses.
Mortal enemy who conquered me in single combat,
in order to flee to your unknown homeland triumphant.

CELESTIAL FREEDOM

Ah the serene forehead!
I would like to know
that the forehead now free of a body which is not air
up above waves where the light exists,
up above strikes skies which generously
give their lives as blue as fresh rain.

Let me, yes, let me.
The heart yearns,
it yearns under earth to perish like a moon,
like the dry moon that is nailed to the ground;
a solid moonset which with one blow is incrusted.

The heart would kill the earth,
it would kill like a love that squeezes or asphyxiates a hated body,
a body that surrenders bleeding alive
while lips or bubbles of death are kissing.

But up above the head escapes.
Sovereign beauty, majesty of the forehead,
serene eastern skin where a sun is etched,
where a sun warmly binds like an arm,
a loved skin, fine, of a naked woman.

Round clear sky in which to live flying,
in which to sing fluttering eyes that shine,
in which to feel blood like blue firmament
that circulates joyously copying free worlds!

SMOKE AND EARTH

You who have traveled the world, tell me
how it is that the pleasure of living
passes by like a fleeting graceful cloud
just like a half-seen breast.

Why, on setting foot on the earth
abandoning the air we wander in,
it hurts like a red-hot iron that melts us
leaving us just like a hesitant smoke.

You are beautiful.   You, distance of the land I contemplate from here
when, elevated like a purified fleece,
I am smoke or memory of stifled suffering
which tangles in the wind like dark eyes.

I am the trace of an ended pain.
I am greeting to the purest atmosphere,
to that transparent blue which like one single hand
feels a silent smoke on its eternal skin.

I am all that never obstructs the flying birds,
all that splits in two when crossed by a heart,
when pierced by a hot ball of feather
unaware that a body is vulnerable.

You, vague wish that crosses like a finite desire,
that makes the air recall the movement of a heart,
so that the penultimate waves can be felt on the cheeks,
the waves that come to die only on our eyelashes.

You, air freed from the land where a man's bones
are like gentle rain, like an inaudible moan,
like peace or convulsion which has finally ended
when purple lips are now earth and not kiss.

You, land who still resemble a beautiful body when you clench in a fist,
when, falling pulverized from mortal fingers,
you fall like a vague impotent desire, like a silent answer
to a question as hermetic as a kiss on the lips.

You, majestic land who sometimes with the color of eyes,
reflect celestial birds or a cloud,
reflect that sweet spasm of love
with which an extended body caresses the sand.

Vague image of life or happiness, lasting land,
powerful love that turns in one's arms,
star or round word pronounced by lips
in the very moment perhaps of a kiss we do not hear.

FINAL FIRE

But you, come here, listen to me and be quiet.
You are as small as a small jasmine.
The world burns up, don't you feel how it crackles?
But you are tiny.   You weigh scarcely as much as a sleeping heart.
Your blond hair still wants to wave in the wind.
It wants to be the image of breezes in air or lead,
not knowing the flames that crackle so near.

Love, love, the world is coming to an end.
You are as beautiful as the hope of living yet.
As the certainty of loving you day after day.
Tender like that sweet abandon on June nights,
when a summer begins confident of its skies.

Little girl small or sweet who are love or life,
a promise when the fire nears,
a promise of living, of living in May,
without having those flames which are burning the world
reduce you to nothing, oh tiniest among fires.

You are going to die perhaps the way the light dies,
that weak candle which the flames assume.
You are going to die like wings not of a bird
but of a weak light held between fingers.

Under the last kisses another light goes away.
I do not ask you for love, nor do I ask your life.
I shall stay here with you.   We are light united,
that sword in the shadow which motionless will burn up,
will melt united when the flames come.

INHUMAN WORLD

A sea.   A moon.
An emptiness without hours beneath a vanished sky.
A clamor that escapes not heeding the blood.
A light in the west as fast as air.

Everything flies ceaselessly on the way to the east,
on the way to the fast air towards the breast.
There there are no birds but the clouds roll on
as cautious as the foam of a total ocean.

There, there, among the clear joys
of that blue unknown by mortal men,
there beats a sea which is not blood,
a water which is not anvil,
a green or delirium
of all that raises up in the end with its wings extended.

There man does not exist.
High eagles touch their inhuman limit.
Warm feathers escape from empty talons,
and a sun which beats alone distantly sends forth
golden waves, but never to the pulse.

Light, gold, shaded carmin beats.
A branch or fire rises up like an arm of roses.
A hand does not exist, but it would bind the sky
seeking blindly the rosy tumescence.

Immensity of the air.   There is no voice that clamors.
Nightless profundity where life is life.
Where death escapes like finite death,
with a fist clamoring against the dry walls.

No!
Man is very far.   High wall of blood.
Man screams mute his wooded heart.
His blood dripping, his sadness weighty.
Covered by the fabric of a fallen sky
distantly man dries out against a wall.

TORMENT OF LOVE

I loved you, I loved you, for your eyes, your lips, your throat your voice,
your heart inflamed in violence.
I loved you like my fury, my furious destiny,
my darkness without dawn, my moon smashed.

You were beautiful.   You had large eyes.
Large doves, swift talons, high eagles most powerful. . .
You had that fullness through a gleaming sky
where the roar of worlds is not a kiss on your mouth.

But I loved you as the moon loves blood,
as the moon seeks blood in the veins,
as the moon supplants blood and runs furiously
through veins inflamed with yellow passions.

I don't know what death is, if one kisses the mouth.
I don't know what it is to die.   I don't die.   I sing.
I sing dead and decayed like a brilliant bone,
radiant before the moon like purest crystal.

I sing like the flesh, like the hard stone.
I sing your fierce teeth without words.
I sing its lonely shadow, its saddest shadow
over the sweet earth where grass becomes gentle.

Nobody cries.   Don't look at this face
where the tears don't live, don't breathe.
Don't look at this stone, this flame of iron,
this body that resounds like a metallic tower.

You had hair, sweet curls, glances and cheeks.
You had arms and not limitless rivers.
You had your form, your precious frontier, your sweet margen of shaken flesh.
Your heart was like a winged flag.

But your blood no, your life no, your evil no!
Who am I to beg the moon for my death?
Who am I to resist the winds, to feel the wounds of its frenetic knives,
to let them wet its marble drawing
like a hard statue bloodied by the storm.

Who am I not to listen to my voice in the thunderbursts
nor my arm of bone with the sign of lightening,
nor the bloody rain that tinges the grass that is born
between my feet bitten by a river of teeth?

Who am I, who are you, who knows you?
Whom do I love, oh you, beautiful mortal,
shining lover, radiant breast;
whom, whom do I love, what shadow, what flesh,
what decomposed bones that like flowers inebriate me?

GUITAR OR MOON

Guitar like moon.
Is it the moon or its blood?
It is a tiny heart that has escaped
and over the woods goes leaving its sleepless blue music.

A voice or its blood,
a passion or its horror,
a fish or dry moon
that darts in the night spattering valleys.

Deep hand or threatened anger.
The moon is red or yellow?
No, it is not an eye injected in the fury
of witnessing the limits of the small earth.

Hand which through the skies seeks life itself,
seeks the pulse of a bleeding sky,
swims in the entrails among the oid planets
that miss the guitar which gives light in the night.

Pain, pain of abreast no one defines,
when the beasts feel their hair stand on end,
when they feel soaked in the cold light
that seeks their skins like a chimerical hand.

ANGRY LOVE

I loved you, I loved you!
You had clear eyes.
Why did I love you?
You had large eyes.
I loved you the way one loves the furious light of a vibrant noon,
summer that hurts like a red whip.

I loved you for your sterile hair,
for your stone hands,
for your body of herbs combed by the wind,
for your tear tracing in newly formed clay.

I loved you like a shadow
like light, like the sound of doors slammed shut by thunder.
Like the hard lightning which hesitates in the hands
and reaches our breast like raw destiny.

I loved you, I loved you, most beautiful, like the inaccessible mountain
that lifts its raw mass against a lost sky.
There no birds come, nor do clouds reach
its cold mute peak unknown by a volcano.

I loved you most of all perhaps like one loves the sea,
like one loves a beach all alive with lips,
like one loves all the sand which quivering
rises up tossed by a thirsty hurricane.

I loved you like the calcareous bed the sea leaves when it retreats,
like the profound abyss where fishes rot,
bare rock where death dreams
a veil as restful as sea green.

You were the light; the anger, the blood, the cruelty, the lie you were.
You, life that creaks in the bones,
flowers sending forth by fistfuls their aromas.
Birds that enter through the eyes and blind
the man, nude upon the earth, who looks.

You, the band of gazelles, their shadow.
You the meditative river or its name and foam.
You the roaring lion and his sterile mane,
his stalking claw that has adored flesh.

I love you; I loved you, I loved you!
I have loved you.
I shall love you the way the body without skin bleeds,
like the last pure stripping of the flesh
that feeds the rivers reddened by anger.

FALLEN MOON

Darkness trembling,
darkness or voice that numbers men,
turmoil of the somber air.

It is the moon, hair or blackness of night;
moon, mordant moon, terrible eye that does not shine,
because it looks within, abyss of the night,
the way dull steel that rolls looks.

There are no moans.
In vain the trees raise up their tops and their nests.
In vain roots send forth their music.
In vain the tentacular entrails seethe
like thick serpents that adore lips.

The night does not cry.
The moon, like a dress or the flesh, like the blackness of bronze,
like the beautiful coal that kisses in the fire,
like the black snow, the only one that does not melt;

The moon, trackless, rolls like doubt,
imitating a pain, a farewell to kisses,
imitating a sadness revealed by dropping the head on the breast,
feigning that lily torn off by the wind;

The bloody moon, imitating a furious negative,
rolls through a land longing to be sky.
It sticks in the sand like a severed hand
which held in its fingers a broken ring.

But the sea's lips can still kiss
(submissive skin of the moon as black as blood).
Fingers can kiss, as pale as birds,
always silent blackbirds under the dark plumage.

Moon of fire or flesh cut by pain,
hand in sand, or flower that straightens without wind,
moon that grows on land, as black as blood,
which only the sea still reaches like light!

THE SKIES

In the middle of the seas and in the high spheres,
under the deep bed of the powerful sea,
seek life perhaps like an unstable flash,
deep darkness for a single breast.

Perhaps the world beats beneath the hard waters,
perhaps there is blood, perhaps a weak heart does not move them.
They weigh very high on a breast with life
that dreams blue skies faintly.

Robust the sea rises without wings to love you,
on gradual sky where no ones has lived.
Robust the sea sends forth its nervous foam
and projects its clear, its vibrant morning stars.
Robust, alien, like a titan it holds up
a whole sky or a breast of love in its arms.

But no.   Clearly, very high, the skies
do not move, do not hang, do not weigh, do not gravitate.
Luminous, without stain, they don't beat like a sea;
but they never smile or slip.   They don't fly.

To the eyes skies are wings with their own edges.
They are kisses with their lips, or wells kiss by kiss.
For hands they are dough that are reviewing life,
as hard as horizons that pulse with blood.

They are that sad ear where remotely
the world moans locked in air, in pure air.
But the sweet glass that other lips review
give their cold of life, of death among suns.

I know it.   For inhuman fires, crystals
only lock up muscles, hearts without anybody.
They are suns or they are moons.   Their name matters not.
They are light or snow or death for lifeless men.

THE POET

For you, who know how the stone sings,
and whose delicate pupil knows now of the weight of a mountain on a sweet eye,
and how the resonant clamor of the forests slumbers smooth one day in our veins;

for you, poet, who felt in your breath
the brutal charge of the celestial birds,
and in whose words the powerful wings of eagles fly as fast
as the back of the warm fishes flash without sound:

hear this book that I send to your hands
with a sign of jungle,
but where suddenly a freshest drop of dew flashes on a rose,
or the desire of the world is seen beating,
sadness that like a sorrowful eyelid
closes the west and hides the sun like a darkened tear,
while the immense fatigued forehead
feels a lightless kiss, a long kiss,
mute words spoken by the dying world.

Yes, poet; love and pain are your kingdom.
Mortal flesh yours, that, snatched by the spirit,
burns in the night or rises in the potent noon,
immense prophetic tongue that licking the skies
illuminates words that bring death to men.

The youth of your heart is not a beach
where the sea charges with its broken foam,
teeth of love that biting the borders of the earth,
roar sweet to beings.

It is not that waking ray that suddenly threatens you,
illuminating for an instant your naked forehead,
in order to plunge into your eyes and set you afire, burning
space with your life which is consumed with love.

No.   That light that in the world
is not an ultimate ash,
light that never abates like dust on lips,
it is you, poet, whose hand and not moon
I saw in the sky one night shining.

A robust breast that reposes pierced by the sea
breathes like the immense celestial tide
and opens its welcoming arms and touches, caresses
the extreme limits of the earth.

Then?
Yes, poet; throw away this book that tries to enclose in its pages a burst of sun,
and look at the light face to face, head leaning on rock,
while your remotest feet feel the last kiss of the west
and your hands raised up sweetly touch the moon,
and your hair hanging down leaves a wake in the stars.

GODDESS

Asleep across the tiger,
lies her light tress.
Look at her form.   It breathes
across the beautiful skin,
tranquil, majestic.
Who can dare, who alone
would now place his lips
on the joyous light,
almost human, that dreams?
Look at her there.   How alone!
How untouched!   Touchable?
Almost divine, lightly
her breast lifts, pauses,
straightens, falls; she moans
like love.   And a tiger
proudly bears her
like the Hircanian sea,
where she would float spacious,
happy, never offered.

Ah, mortals!   No, never;
nude, never yours.
Across the skin now incandescent
look at her, free: she is goddess.

THE POETS

The poets, you ask?

I saw a flower broken
by the breeze.   The silent
clamor of petals
falling ruined
from their perfect dreams.
Vast love without delirium
under the flying light,
while the eyes look at
a tremor of doves
which inscribe an assumption!
I saw, I saw other wings.
Vast wounded wings.
Angels exiled
from their celestial origin
were sleeping on the earth
their highest paradise.
Immense hard dreams
still powerful
were revealed solid
on their most white foreheads.
Who looked at those worlds,
fertile island of a dream,
diamond purity
where love struggles?
Who saw clouds flying
long arms, flowers,
caresses, the night
underfoot, the moon
like a breast pulsing?
Angels without rest
tinge their lucid wings
with a dawnless rouge,
among green valleys.
A love, noon,
plummets vertical
permanent in the nude
shoulders of the lover.
Girls are happy
rivers; their foam
--continuous hands--ties
to their necks flowers
of a light like a sigh

among beautiful words.
The kisses, the heartbeats,
the silent birds,
everything is there, in the breasts
most secret, hard,
which continuously surprise
some eternal lips.
What a tender accent reigns
in the shadowless words
of smooth skins,
the gazelle without name,
a very sweet deer,
lifts its answer
on its forehead for the day!
Oh, the mystery of air
that gets entangled in forms
inexplicably,
like foam without master!
Mysterious angels,
human burning, raise
pensive cupolas
over the fresh waves.
Their laborious wings
move a fickle wind,
which below touches loving
foreheads of the air.
And the earth holds up
naked feet, columns
love would exalt,
temples of fertile joy,
revealed by the moon.
Bodies, souls or sudden
lights, that sing
by the sea, with
lyres alone, almost celestial.

Who saw that solid world,
who battered with his feathers
that radiant wind
that dies on some lips
giving life to men?
What mysterious legion,
angels in exile,
is continuously arriving
invisible to the eyes?
No, don't ask; hush.
The city, its mirrors,

its white voice, its cold
unburied cruelty,
does not know those wings.

You ask, ask. . .

IT IS NOT ENOUGH

But the light of the sun is not enough,
no, it is not enough, nor its warm breath.
The dark mystery of a glance is not enough.
The noisy fire of the woods was scarcely enough one day.
I learned of the sea.   But it isn't enough either.

In the middle of life, on the edge of the stars themselves,
mordant, always sweet in their restless edges,
I felt my forehead light up.
It was not sadness, no.   The world is sad;
but the immense invading happiness of the universe
also reigned in the pale days.

It was not sadness.   A remote message
from an invisible light was modulating some lips,
airily, on pale waves,
waves of a sea intangible to my hands.

A cloud with weight, a cloud charged perhaps with stellar thought,
fleeting on earth, was stopping over the waters,
perhaps a celestial envoy from distant universes
which for one moment stops its passage through the ether.

I saw a forehead being sketched,
a divine forehead: cleft by a luminous wrinkle,
it crossed an instant pregnant with a sombre thought.
I saw a purple flash cross through it, I saw some eyes
shine charged with an infinite grief,
and I saw the cloud depart, dense, dark, closed,
silent, toward the pensive sunset without barriers.

The high sky stayed as if empty.
My scream echoed in the unvaulted hollow
and was lost, like my thought that flew off coming apart,
like a sob upwards, toward the desolate emptiness, toward the hole.

On the earth my form fell.   The skies were
only my awareness, absolute solitude.
I felt on my flesh an emptiness of God,
and without ever looking upwards, ever, I plunged my forehead into the sand
and alone I kissed the earth, the dark, lonely
desperate earth that was welcoming me.

This way I wept over the world.
What pale light, what spectral waking emptiness,
what absence of God on my fallen head
was keeping limitless vigil over my convulsed body?
Oh mother, mother, only in your arms I feel
my misery!   Only on your breast martyrized by my weeping
I surrender my form, only in you I vanish.
These limits that oppress me,
this clay which would be born of the sea,
that here was left on your beaches,
your creation, your work, your light,
lifeless she asks you for her glorious fusion,
she asks only you, untouched mother,
my mother of warm darkness,
breast alone where the void reigns,
my love, my love, already you, you alone.

Still I would like, mother,
with my head resting on your lap,
to turn my forehead toward the sky
and to look upwards, toward the light, toward the pure light,
and feeling your warmth, lying sweetly on your lap,
to contemplate the blue, the smiling hope,
the promise of God, the imagined loving forehead.
How good from you, from your warm earthy flesh,
to watch the pure waves of the beneficent divinity!
To see the light dawn in the east, and in the stormy pregnant cloud
to contemplate one instant the purest divine forehead burst into light,
and those immense beneficent eyes
where the world raised up wants to be copied whole
and be rocked in a swaying of sea, of whole stellar sea,
compiler of stars, of morning stars, of suns,
while universal music sounds, already pure forehead,
radiant love, beautiful light, happiness without limits!

This way, mother well-loved,
you well can know--you know, I feel your secret kiss of wisdom--
that the sea may not be enough, the woods may not be enough,
a dark glance full of human mystery,
may not be enough; love, mother, may not be enough,
just as the world may not be enough.

Mother, mother, on your beautiful breast
tenderly lying, let me tell you like this
my secret; look at my tear
kissing you; mother you who still nourish me,
mother whose deep wisdom sustains me, my offering.

THE POET SINGS FOR EVERYONE

I

There is everyone, and you are watching them pass.
Ah, yes, there, how you would like to join them and recognize yourself!

The furious whirlwind within the heart drives you mad.
Frenetic mass of pain, sprinkled
against those silent interior walls of flesh.
And then in an ultimate effort you decide.   Yes, they pass.
Everyone is passing.   There are children, women.   Serious men.   Certain
*   mourning, glances.*
And a single mass, a unique being, intensely together files by.
And you, with tight heart, convulsed by your solitary pain, in an ultimate
*   effort you plunge in.*
Yes, at last, how you are and find yourself!
There serenely in the wave you surrender yourself.   Quietly you drift.
And you go tightly pushed, like rocked, gentled.
And you hear a dense sound, like a muffled canticle.
It is thousands of hearts that make a single heart that carries you.

II

A single heart that carries you.
Give up your own pain.   Distend your own contracted heart.
A single heart runs through you, a single beat rises to your eyes,
powerfully invades your body, lifts your breast, makes you wave your hands
*   while now you move forward.*

And if you stand straight an instant, if an instant you raise your voice,
I know well what you sing.
That which from all the dark almost infinite bodies has joined together
                                                    and flashed,
which through bodies and souls is suddenly freed in your scream,
it is the voice of those who carry you, the voice true and raised
in which you can hear yourself, in which you, with surprise, recognize yourself.
The voice which through your throat, from all the scattered hearts,
rises up cleanly in the air.

III

And for all ears.   Yes.   Look how they hear you.
They are listening to themselves.   They are listening to a single voice
                                                    that sings them.
The very mass of the song, they move like a wave.
And you submerged, almost dissolved, like a knot of their being you know yourself.
The voice that carries them sounds.   It lies like a road.
All feet are treading on it.
They are treading on it beautifully, they are engraving it with their flesh.
And it unfolds and offers, and the whole mass gravely files on.
Like a mountain it climbs.   It is the path of those who march.
And it ascends to the clear peak.   And the sun opens up on their foreheads.
And at the peak, with its grandeur, everyone is now singing.
And it is your voice that expresses them.   Your voice collective and raised.
And a sky of power, completely existent,
now with majesty makes the whole echo of man.

THE DREAM

   There are moments of solitude
when the heart realizes, astounded, that it does not love.
We have just raised up, tired: the day dark.
Someone is sleeping, innocent, still on that bed.
But perhaps we sleep. . .   Ah no: we move.
And we are sad, quiet.   The rain, out there insists.
Morning of slow fog, impious.   How alone we are!
We look through the windowpanes.   The clothing, tumbled;
the air, heavy; the water, sounding.   And the room,
frozen in this hard winter which, outside, is different.

And so you remain quiet, your face in your palm.
Your elbow on the table.   The chair, in silence.
And the only sound is the paused breathing of someone,
of the one who, over there, serene, beautiful is sleeping
and dreaming that you do not love her, and you are her dream.

WE DON'T DIE

Lovers don't have a vocation for dying.   « We shall die?»
You say that to me, looking at me absorbed with large eyes: «Forever!»
«Forever,» «never»:   words
that we lovers say, not for their empty sense that flows and passes,
but for their hold on the ear, for their harsh plaint and their prolonged
                                                                    vibration,
that ends, now, that gradually ceases. . . , that sweetly goes out like an
                                                    extinction in dreams.

We won't die, will we my love?   We will live each day.
We make vague plans for when old age comes.   And we say:
« You will always be beautiful, and your eyes the same:
ah, the soul there colored, in the tiny pupil,
perhaps in the voice. . . Beyond life's accumulation,
beyond everything which is hiding you
--if that is hiding you, that will not be, that cannot be--I shall know you
                                                    always.»
There you will go forth, through the slender thread of voice, through the
                            never entirely extinguished brilliance of
                                        the green of your eyes,
through the warmth of the recognizable hand, through the silent kisses.
Through the long silence of the two silent bodies, that grope, know each other.
Through the slow continuous whitening of the hair, which one by one I shall
                                                    make mine.
Slow daily minute which like a drop joins us,
binds us.   Drop that falls and wets us; we fell it: it is one.

We two have slowly looked at each other.
How many times you tell me: «Don't remind me of the years!»
Buy you also tell me, at times of closeness and whispering:
«Yes, the years are you, are your love.   We exist!»
Now that nothing changes, that nothing can change, like life itself,
                                        like me, like together. . .
Slow growing of the branch, slow curving, slow extending: slow,

at last, far away, slow bending.   And branch filled with fruit, so laden,
                                              so rich
--so continuously together: like a gift, like being here--
until another hand that may be, that will be, picks it,
more still than like the earth, like love, like a kiss.

FOR WHOM I WRITE

I

For whom do I write?   the chronicler, the journalist or simply the curious
                            used to ask me.
I don't write for the man in the fancy jacket, nor for his angry mustache,
              nor even for his index finger raised up adminishing amidst the
                                              sad waves of music.

Nor for the carriage or for its hidden mistress (behind the glass, like a
                            cold ray, the brilliance of the impertinent).

I write perhaps for the ones who don't read me.   That woman who runs down
                    the street as if she were opening doors for the dawn.

Or that old man who drowses on the bench in that small plaza, while the
              setting sun with love takes him, surrounds him and softly
                                              dissolves him in its lights.

For all those who don't read me, those who don't care about me, but care
                    about me (although they may be unaware of me).

That little girl who as she passes looks at me, companion of my adventure,
                                              living in the world.

And that old woman who sitting at her door has seen life, given birth
                                              to many lives, and tired hands.

I write for the lover; for the one who passed with his anguish in his eyes;
                    for the one who heard him; for the one who on passing did not
        look; for the one who finally fell when he asked and was not heard

For everyone I write.   For those who don't read me above all I write.   One by
one and the crowd.   And for the breasts and for the mouths and
for the ears where, without hearing me,

my word is there.

II

But I write also for the murderer.   For the one who with eyes closed threw
himself on a breast and ate death and nourished himself, and
arose insane.

For the one who reacted like a tower of wrath, and toppled down on the world.

And for the dead women and for the dead children, and for the dying men.

And for the one who carefully opened the gas taps and the whole city perished,
and a mound of cadavers appeared at dawn.

And for the innocent girl, with her smile, her heart, her tender medal,
where an army of ravagers passed.

And for the army of ravagers, which in a final gallop rushed to sink into the
waters.

And for those waters, for the infinite sea.

Oh, not for the infinite.   For the finite sea, with its almost human limitation,
like a lived breast.

(A child now enters, a child bathes, and the sea, the heart of the sea, is in
that pulse).

And for the final glance, for the most limited Final Glance, in whose breast
someone sleeps.

Everyone sleeps.   The murderer and the victim, the ruler and the new born,
the deceased and the damp, the dry of will and the rough like
a tower.

For the threatener and the threatened, for the good and the sad, for the
voice without flesh
and for all the flesh of the world.

For you, man without godhead who, without wanting to see them, are reading
these words

For you and everything that lives in you

I am writing.

THE WORDS OF THE POET

After the dead words, the ones still pronounced or spoken,
what do you expect?   Some flying pages,
more papers scattered.   Who knows?   Some words
undone, like the echo or the light that dies there in the great night.

Everything is deep night.
Dying is forgetting some words spoken
in moments of delight or anger, of ecstacy or abandon,
when, the soul awakened looms in the eyes
more like light than like expert sound.
Expert, since it would be arranged
by virtue of its sound on the open page,
resting on words, or they with sound drench
the air and rest.   Not with supreme virtue,
but yes with an order, infallible, if they want.
Because obedient, they, the words, attain
to their virtue and docile
they pose majestic, under the light they appear
on a human tongue which tries to express them.

And the hand reduces
its movement to finding them,
no: to discovering them, useful, while they shine, they reveal,
when not, disappointed, they vanish.

And so, abandoned at times, they sleep,
residue at the end of an intact fire
which although it died does not forget,
but weak it left its memory, and there it would be.

Everything is deep night.
Dying is forgetting words, springs, glass, couds,
to attain to an order
invisible by day, but certain in the night, in a great abyss.
There the earth, strict,

permits no other love than the whole center.
No other kiss than being it.
No other love than the love that, choked, radiates.

In the deep nights
the abandoned or sleeping words
would find correspondence.
Among flying papers, who knows them or forgets?
Sometime, perhaps, they will resound, who knows?
in a few kindred hearts.

THE YEARS

Are the years their weight or are they their history?   The hardest thing is to go
slowly, even with love, smiling.   And they say: « Young man;
ah, how young you seem. . .»   To seem, not to be?   Language is fitting.
Those surprising figures pass.   Because the eye--which is still alive--looks
and copies the gold of the hair, the rosy flesh, the white of the sudden
                                             ivory.   The laughter is clear
to everyone, and also to him, who lives and hears it.
But the years cast
something like a turbid round clarity,
and he moves within the hated globe.   And he is not visible
or he scarcely is, because he passes by unknown, and stays enveloped.
It is not possible to break the round glass or the air
that perpetual cone that houses something:
even a being who moves and passes by, already invisible.
While the others, free, cross, strike blind.

Because striking blind is emitting life in fresh rays.
but the one who passes alone, protected
by his age, crosses without being sensed.   The air, still.
He hears and feels, because the strange wall
robs him of his light but air is only
for the light that comes, and passes the edge.
Having passed the soul, on foot, the one who lives still crosses.

THE OLD AND THE YOUNG

Some, young, pass by.   There they pass, in succession, alien to the glorious
afternoon that annoints them.
The way those old ones
more slowly go yoked
to that final ray of the setting sun.
They are very aware of the warmth of the fine afternoon.
Slender the sun touches them and they take
its warmth: it is a good--there are so few left!--
and they pass by slowly down that clear path.

It is the first greening of the early season.
A youthful river, rather the childhood of a nearby spring,
and the incipient greening: young oaks,
woods by the port in swift ascent.
Very Swift.   But the old no longer go with its rhythm.
And there the young who are moving forward pass by
without seeing, and go on, without looking at them.
The old look at them.   They are still,
these are, the ones who at the end of life,
on the edge of the end, remain suspended,
without falling, as if forever.
While the youthful shadows pass, they are consumable, unstable,
driven by the thirst that one breath sates.

THE OLD MAN IS LIKE MOSES

Like Moses on the top of the mountain.

Each man can be him
and move the word and lift the arms
and feel how the light sweeps, from his face,
the old dust of the road.

Because there is the sunset.
Look backwards: the dawn.
Ahead: more shadows.   And the lights were pointing!
And he waves his arms and proclaims life,
from his death all alone.

Because like Moses, he is dying.
Not with the useless tablets, and the chisel, and the ray on high,
but with the texts broken on the earth, with the hair
burned, with the ears scorched by the terrible words,
and still breath in his eyes, and in his lungs the flame,
and in his mouth the light.

To die one sunset is enough.
A bit of shadow on the line of the horizon.
A swarming of adolescences, hopes, voices.
And there succession, earth: the limit.
What the others will see.

FINAL FACE

Decadence adds truth, but it doesn't flatter.   Ah, the vicissitude
wil not be avoided, since it is time.
But, yes its painful error, its sad sediment.   Rather its stern visage,
its residue impressed: there horror without mask.
Because the old man is not his mask, but some other lewd nakedness;
beyond the skin it is peering out,
without dignity.   Disorder: what we see is not a face.
That is why, when the old man exhibits his hilarious vision
                                                           he sees himself behind bars,
degraded, the recollection of some living, and there appears
the pointed nose, eaten or gnawed away, the thinning hair,
a mat, the turbid drop that makes up the eye, and the hollow or crack
where the mouth was and is missing.   There a dry
wound still opens and mimicks some sound: a sad bellows.
With hooks grasping the bars, sounds
broken by several large yellow teeth are mouthed,
which, if they exist, belong to another species.   No longer human.
There behind that face remains a cry, a scream
suspended, gesticulation without time. . .
And there behind bars we see the final lie.   No longer life.

THE PAST: PURE VILLAGE

Here in the little house,
three trees in front, the door standing, the sound:
everything persists, or dead,
when I cross.   I remember: «Pure Village.»
Pure of what; of the wind.
Here that child erected
the tremor.   Here he looked at the sand
dead,
the mud like a glove,
the light like his pale cheeks
and the old gold giving
on his hair a kiss
without yesterday.   Today, tomorrow.

The leaves have fallen, or from the earth to the tree
they rose today
and they still feign
passion, being, sound.   And I cross
and they give no shade,
since they are.   And there is no smoke.

To wake.   To live.   I
cannot,
I ought not
remember.   Nothing lives.   Curtain which the wind moves
without existing.   And I am silent.

A TERM

Knowing is not the same as to know.   The one who learned by listening;
the one who suffered or enjoyed;
the one who died all alone.
Everyone walks or runs, but they go slowly always
in the fast wind that drags them there.
They swim against the current, but they retreat,
and carried in the waters while they struggle upstream,
they end up on their backs.
It is the end with everything into which they sink.
Free sea, the dark sea where they rest.

THE ONE WHO WAS

The disconnected moon has burned out
on men.   The entire valley has died.
The shadow invades its memory, and would be
dust imagined, if it existed.   And not fantasy.
Since mineral the earth has anticipated
matter: man has aspired here.
A gold devoured, a wind cold:
that close breath is a cloud.
It wants to last.   There is no stone.   Man loved.

The creature imagined exists.   But it is not enough.
It would not be enough.   Ah, never were it enough.
Love imagined. . .   If there were anyone who could and who might think,
anyone with awakened lights put
his eyes in caution, and dreamt a fire.

Loving is not a fire, but its memory.
Its imagined fire glows.
The moving shadows consumed
--thin, light, like burned paper--
by that voracious mind that no longer has seen.
Thought alone is not visible.
The one who sees is knowing, the one who has died is sleeping.
The one who could have been was not.   Nobody has loved him.
A man entirely retracted, never
were you believed; never created;
never known.
The one who could have loved did not love.   The one who was, has not been.

THE YOUNG

I

Some are looking, slowly.
Dark, almost mineral, quiet,
they would be life, like the stone, and they sing.
The stone sings, the one who has lived sings.
The quiet minerals do not know
what death is, and their dark burning moans in the shadow.

Young are the ones who step slowly.   There are sad ones,
since sadness is youth, or the kiss.
They are numerous, like kisses themselves, and on the lip
the sun does not burn, but it weds.
On the fleshy lip the day lives.
Night passes on them: it is their shadows.
They pass slowly and steal the breeze.
Youth, when it loves, dislocates.
Oh absolute youth.   They are many,
they are like the sea and they come like the wave.
Their waves come arriving.   A continuous sea, without end, assuages
the thirst of the sand or world.   And they
are slow waters, but sure,
and they love
like the sand kisses the one who razes it.
The sea, the sea.   Youth has not flamed, but it burned up.
And on the sands the lucid water stands.

II

Others, more visible, are the one who lives,
who laughs.   The bodies are passing by
Only the light says it.   Complete light,
because light populated.   It is not the ray of the sun that burns and flees,
but the one which, delayed, there is in the flesh
with the whole man in its lucent waving.
All life is light, and it undulates
in the ray: there are the luminous generations
that were, but still live, that still exist.
And there in the light, like light, they come to you
like the youth itself of the world.

III

More young are seen.   They are the not dead,
because not born.
They are the ones thought.
Not in the night or idea,
in the dawn, their image,
like their thought they appear or they are.   The light
stays happy, ah, not touched,
because
the one who wasn't born doesn't stain.   Everything lights,
believed: oh immaculate thought.
Beautiful, like the intact thought alone:
a glimmer.

IF ANYONE HAD TOLD ME

If once you could
have told me what you didn't tell.
On this almost perfect night, next to the vault,
on this cool summer night.
When the moon has burned;
the chariot burned up; the great star plunged down.
And in the nocturnal sky, thick with hollow lividities,
there is only pain,
because there is memory, and solitude, and oblivion.
And even the leaves reflected fall.   They fall and they last.   They live.

If anyone had told me.
I am not young and I exist.   And this hand moves.
It slithers down this shadow, it explains its poisons,
its mysterious doubts before your living body.
A long time ago the cold
had a birthday.   The moon slipped into waters.
The sea closed up, and turned green in its brilliance.
For a long time, a long long time,
it has slept.   The waves become quiet.
The foam sounds the same, only of silence.
It is like a sad fist
and it grabs the dead and explains them,
and shakes them, and bashes them against the fierce rocks.

And it splatters them.   Because the dead, when bashed,
when brained against the artful granite,
splatter.   They are matter.
And they don't stink.   They are even deader,
and they scatter and cover, and they make no noise.

They are dead finished.
Perhaps still not begun.
Some have loved.   Others talked a lot.
And they explain themselves.   Useless.   Nobody listens to the living.
But the dead are quiet with juster silences.

If you had told me.
I knew you and I have died.   The only thing lacking is for a fist,
a wretched fist to bash me,
to raise me up and brain me,
and for my voice to be scattered.

CAVE OF NIGHT

Look at it.   Here kissing you, I say it.   Look at it.
In this dark cave, look, look at
my kiss, my final darkness that covers with definitive
night
your luminous dawn
that breaks
in black, and like a sun within me announces to me
another truth.   Which you, deep, ignore.
From your being my clarity comes to me whole
from you, my funeral dawn that opens into night.
You, my nocturnity that, light, blinds me.

NEAR TO DEATH

It is not sadness that life points to
or nears, when the steps are many, and they last.
There the wilderness, here the glassy city,
or it is a reflection of that very long sun
that plots responses
long distance
for lips that, living, live,
or recall.
The majesty of memory is air
afterwards, or before.   Facts are a sigh.
That curtain of yellow silk
that a breath moves, and another light puts out.

THE LIMIT

Enough.   It is not insisting to look at the long shining of your eyes.   There,
to the end of the world.
I looked and obtained.   I contemplated, and it was passing.
The dignity of man is in his death.
But the temporary shining adds
color, truth.   The light, once thought, deceives.
Enough.   In the current of light--your eyes--I put

may faith.   Through them I saw, I would live.
Today when I tread my end, I kiss these limits.
You, my limitation, my dream.   Be!

PRESENT, AFTERWARDS

Enough.   After life there is no kiss and I feel you.
                                        Your deceased lips suggest to me
that I live.   Or I am the one who calls you.
To place my lips on your idea is to feel you
a proclamation.   Oh yes, terrible, you exist.
I am the one who expired, the one who pronounced your name, like form
while I was dying.

Born of me;
here present because I have said you.

OBLIVION

Your end is not like an empty cup
that must be drained.   Throw off the shell, and die.

That is why slowly you lift in your hand
a brilliance or its mention, and your fingers burn,
like a sudden snow.
It is and was not, but it was and is silent.
The cold burns and in your eyes is born
its memory.   To remember is obscene;
worse: it is sad.   To forget is to die.

With dignity it died.   Its shadow crosses.

SOUND OF WAR

Soldier.

Here I arrived.   Here I stay.   It is sad
to know that the day is embodied in night.
I looked at the light eternal in some beautiful eyes.
How far away now!   Here in the jungle I perceive
the only light, and I live.   Since I do not know
here where I come from.   It is the tenacious
birds that live after, that
fly over.   Here at my feet lianas
boil, and they feel that the earth is everything, and nothing
is different.   The sky is not distinct.
The bird is earth and flies.
Heron the same as hawk.   What bird
ghosts, what screeching
ghosts!   The water passes and spreads.
Here my mineral body today can
live.   I am stone since I exist.

Witch doctor.

I was left alone.   The village is razed.
Ah, the wretched
conquistador passed.   Shrapnel and, worse, poison
I saw in the horrible glance.   And they were young.
How many times I dreamed of a sigh
like a sweet death.   In my brews
I put the belladonna of non-being, and I learned how
to sleep, terrible ultimate science.
But today it did me no good.   With fixed eye
I watched and I looked, and dry
an eye saw the rain, and it was red.
Paly and dry,
and bloody inside, it blinded.

Soldier.

I am not asleep.   I don't know if I die or sleep.
In this wound is living, and now
it alone is life.
I had some lips that meant.
A body that stood erect, an arm stretched out,
like hands that apprehended: things,
objects, beings, hopes, smoke.

I dreamed, and the hand drew the dream,
the desire.   I groped.   The one who gropes lives.   The one who knows has died.
Only my thought lives now.
Therefore I die.   Because I no longer look,
but I know.   Young I was.   And without age, I end.

Witch doctor.

Since I saw I looked.   The blood was not a river,
but its painful thought.
Blood lives when imprisoned it fights
to spurt out.   But if it spurts, it dies.
Like a castle where the beauty
is a prisoner and a sweet knight
opens the gate and goes out: light kills.
Just like blood, in which destiny errs,
since if it shines forth it dies.   Ah, what an incredible
mystery.   Only on some lips colored
as if through a blind, can the form of blood
be divined.   And the lover
can kiss and imagine, without seeing it!

Bird.

Who speaks here in the night?   They are human
poisons.   I am now old and I hear little,
but I don't confound the song of the lark
with the hoarse movement of the poor breast.
I look and all around there is hardly any air now
for my wings.   Nor branch for my rest.
What destruction occurred?   I recognize nothing.
Nature fled.   What is this?   And I fly
in an air that kills.
Lethal ash in which to float, and I die.

Soldier.

What horrible thirst.   In dry earth, nothing.
I am stretched out and I only see stars.
The hole of my breast breathes
like a brutal error.   I think, I don't speak.
I feel.   One day feeling would be living.
Perhaps today I feel because I'm dying.
And the last word be: I felt.

Witch doctor.

*I walk groping.   Among stones I walk
or among scattered limbs?   Cold a heel or is it a broken forehead?
How noisy a fragment that is alone:
Beyond death something lives,
a remains, in its own life.   And I walk, I put aside
that other life by itself that I don't understand.*

Soldier.

*I someone would come...I cannot speak.   I
cannot scream.   I was young and I looked, I burned,
I touched, I sounded.   Man sounds.   But silent, I die.
And here the stars already went out,
since my eyes no longer know them.
Only the air of the breast sounds.   The rasping
within me breathes through the wound,
as if through a mouth.   Useless mouth.
Recent, and made only
for dying.*

Witch doctor.

*The war was because it is being.   Those err
who name it.   They are worth nothing and are merely words
that drag you, a dust shadow,
smoke exploded, human as you turn out
like an idea dead beyond nothingness.
Where the belladonna of your sleep, juice
for sleeping, if everything has died and I see
only that the light thinks?   No, there is no life,
merely this thought in which I end:
The thought of the light without men.*

Lark.

*Everything is quiet and everything is deserted.
And the dawn is born, and silent.
I passed like a stone and I ended in the sea.*

THE OLD LOVERS

He.

   It is not exhaustion that impels me
to silence.   The afternoon is beautiful, and it lasts.

She.

   The nightingale is seen in the night.   I do not listen.
The wind dishevels this hair.   But not mine.
And the moon is cold.

He.

   Hear the earth
how it moans long.   They are steps, or their idea.   I cannot
say even what lives in the breast.
Live your dream and look at your hair.   Is it the hair that waves
when I think it?   Or is it the night all alone?
Oh you never seen and always found.
The one not listened to--and always silenced.
From your continuous sound I go living.
I lived the years, oh no, I lived the lights.
I lived your mysterious lights, and behold me
blind with you.   My eyes exhausted
do not see.   My arms do not reach you.
After I lived you, like a life, alone
I ought to be, since I look and I grope, and no one,
nothing.   The blind eye sees a cosmos.   Would not see!

She.

   I well know that is a voice I hear.   Nearby,
here by my side.   Tell me.   Sing
the forest.   The nightingale invites.   The wind passes.
Is this my hair?   Always branches.
The wind is high.   The stringy hair hangs.
Take me, clear wind, take and flee.

He.

  The sea tells me there is a presence.
The solitude of man is not its kiss.
The one who lives loved, the one who knows has already lived.
This foam that whips my face
is it foam, is it my dream?   I extended an arm
and I feel the truth frozen.   You do not deceive,
thought alone
which is my whole company.   The solitude of man is in kisses.
Were they kisses, or have I been?   I am, or were they never?   I am
                                                  the one who doubts.

She.

  I smile, since my teeth are,
still, echo and mirror, and the light strikes them.
Existing is shining.   I am the one who responds.
It does not matter that this forest does not heed.
My stars, its branches, sing faithful.

He.

  Thought lives more than man.
The one who lives, dies.   The one who died, still breathes.
Grief is not possible, and it grows.
Like the forehead between the hands lasts.
Ah, forehead alone.   You now alone, all of life.

She.

  But the bird delights its passage.   I listen,
purest singer.   Through me you have flown
and here in the forest your name is communion.
My name is you.   I am you, my bird.

He.

  What a solitude of extinct lights.
I do not see the living tongue, still I feel
its ash on my skin, and it licks, and it lies.
No: Truth decides and expression confides.
Its cold tongue speaks to me here, and, silent,
is the one who tells me: «love,» and I exist.

She.

  The night is young.   The hours are brief,
because they are beautiful.   It is the pure

stars who say it.   They proclaimed
that the world does not age.   Their beautiful
perpetual light is in my eyes: they also shine.

He.

What insistence in living.   I only understand it
as formulation of the impossible: the real
world.   Here in the shadow I understand
definitively that if I loved I was not.
Being is not loving, and the one who is deceived dies.

She.

What a long wait!   I am getting tired now.
Here he agreed to return.   Years or days,
perhaps a minute.   But how long!
I am getting tired now.   The stars say: Now it is your time.
How do you doubt?
I do not doubt.   I sing.   I have been beautiful;
I am, I mean, since I was.   I am beautiful because being,
and I await.   Here we agreed, next to the forest.
He left, I wait for him.   Oh, come.

He.

No one moves, if he walks, and the one who
flows, stopped.   Here the sea undermines
or undermined, my faith.   Life.   I see. . .
I see nothing, I know nothing.   It is soon, or never.

She.

With clear dress I prepared myself.   Come back,
come back soon!   That is how I heard him.   Spring was
in its splendor.   Oh, how many springs
here wating.   Why, why has he delayed
so long!   Life motionless, like the always motionless
most fixed light of the star, says
that light is young, and I continue in it.
The forest fled.   But, another forest is born.
And, my clear star, I sing you,
I reflect you.   We are. . .   We wait.

He.

The majesty of this silence augers
that the thought can be the world

Living, thinking.   Feeling is different.
Feeling is light,
blood is light.   That is why the day goes out.
But darkness can think, and it dwells in
a cosmos like a cranium.   And it does not end;
like the stone.   It thinks, therefore it exists.
Oh thought, in stone; you, life.

She.

He was light like the wind, and he came
and he spoke to me: «I am the one who loves you, I am the one who has felt you.
I shall never forget you.   Loving you is life,
feeling you is life.»   That is what he said to me, and he left.
But I know it.   Like an enduring flash
he is there, and he came, and if he passed, he stays.
Here I wait for him.   I am old. . .   Ah no, young I mean,
young I am, since I feel.   The one who feels lives, and lasts.

He.

I conceive only your truth.   Mine
I am not knowing.   To you I speak, and I do not know
if I am saying.   To whom I say
does not matter.   As it doesn't matter either what I say
or what I die.   If I love or if I have lived.

She.

I shall not live.   Dawn is being born.
Is it night?   The forest is here?   Is it the moon
or is it you, my star, who tends
to disappear?   The day breaks.   Clarity
makes me darkness.   Am I the one who is being born
or the one who flickers?   The one who waits or the one who sleeps?
I speak, and the light moves forward.   The stars
go out.   Ah, I do not see myself.

He.

Darkness is all
truth, without incidents

to belie it.   Here I lived, and I have died.
Be quiet: knowing is loving.   To know, to die.
I doubted.   Never is love life.

She.

   He is about to arrive, and I am ending.   I waited so long, and I have died.
I knew what it is to love because I lived daily.
I does not matter.   He has come now.   And here laid out I say
that living is loving, and always I knew.

He.

   Be quiet.   The one who speaks listens.   And the one who was silent
has already spoken.

THE YOUNG LOVERS

He (outside the garden)

   I am young and I am knowing.   I did not know and I am old.
These walls enclose the truth I divine.
Nubile in the grove, silent in the lights,
it passes like the breath of a tranquil virgin.
And it is she.   I have not seen her.   I glimpsed her: I am knowing her.
And this garden hides from me behind its walls her form,
not her radiance--for, blind, i grope my jail--.
I was born in this city crowned with towers,
behind a driving river that permits other flight.
Wings, kisses or music tremble over its waves
an instant, and the waters assume them and hide.
Garden where she is born and dies in its other sky,
like a light lost from a ray in the west.
Each morning, and she lives.   What a sensation of dawn!
Each night and she sleeps, without my dark lips.

She (in the garden)

   I beg the beautiful light for a name and the light is silent.
Among the roses, birds, like another light I wait.
My name?   Never a lip spoke it in beautiful chrism.
Nor will speak it.   Who Knows!   Beneath the light the day.

He.

Here in another grove my destiny dawns.
I know it.   Life was
of luminous flesh, incarnation of the world.
But the light should not be touched.

She.

Ah, the sealed rose,
that first silence on which I put my lips.

He.

Garden of torments where love persists.
Garden of knives with which you threaten the heart.
I raise myself up and I swear by my love, by my life.
A cruel and unknown god pursues the man alone.
But nobody has seen him.   Solitude, who are you?
Shadow of a body or kiss, pure exhaustion wounded
where my lips touch, not its truth, its death.
God of a light that ends, while my lips I feel
burned, no, ended, by love without day.

She.

With the day I was born.   With the foam of the world.
A petal sealed for my new lips.
I am a child and a moon is reborn, dies, is born.
Ah, what firmest dawn!
Quiet, you mad birds who pecking my lips
place kisses or laughter or blue plumage.
For the nightingale amazes me with its longest passion
like a single note for the nocturnal garden.
Lark: the morning blackbird: the day grows.
And in the night now human I hear the clear voices
of children who shout or sing or live.
Sun I feel under my feet at dawn.
Sun I tread upon and it shines under my naked feet.
I raise my arms: the light rises. Ah noon
beautiful and now complete under my fresh roses.

He.

But I was born alone.   Soon the world was sleeping.
The shadows of other men like hope or doubt
erupted quiet but urgent, and vile.
What did I see?   With finger on lips it passed and was alone.

Then the plain, the valleys.   The eyes of the deer.
Horn or ostentatious sky.   And in its cradle the moon.
Lyre opened of the world, wind like body, numen,
silky skin or mourning for the vast fields
where force rules like light, strict.

She.

   I knew by not knowing.   Because the one who looks learns.
But I did not see a lip, but rather a star alone.

He.

   I am knowing my destiny, although the wall hides it.
I feel its mass and, blind, I proclaim its radiance.
I do not know, but I am knowing.   The one who remembers is the one who is dying.
I live and I feel the kisses through the day's vocation.
Garden of torments which you aim at the heart.
Garden of knives with which you threaten the heart.
Swords like flowers for cold lips,
and flowers like swords for the burning coal.
I was born for the world.   For loving.   I have not moaned.
I rule since I exist.   I plunge down, since I love.
And this mouth now feels all the fire of the world
like another flower suddenly with which to inebriate life.
To smell, to live.   I come.   Who calls me?   Those walls
are smoke or chimera.   Struck down, there has opened
the garden or life, or earth, or death.

THAT SWAN'S WAY

Swan.

   It is not road: arrival.   Since the one who doubts is the one who arrives.
It is I, with my monocle, who listens to other lights.
Not of stars, for I never caught their brilliance.

Marcel.

You were a chimera in whom I rested.
A shadow, or I merely looked at you in the mirror,
while I felt looking at you
that a ghost does not die
while it loves.   You lived?

Swan.

Clothing is what loves.   Not the one who sounds in the dark.
It is not I, nor is it my name.   It is only the glance
that knows what it forgets, or remembers if it dies.
I am who I was, if that is being it; but in conscience and alone.

Marcel.

When you were crossing over the carpet of a lady
the multitude far off was sleeping like a world,
but my hand placed on a shoulder only
a diamond, a pearl, while you were smiling.
Wise of what?   Of the world?   Of its unpunished mask?

Swan.

Like a frock coat I passed, without my mask, alone,
before the grandiose mirror I lived in, and I loved it.
Since if I loved it was for that: because I didn't love and I knew it.
To live: only an excuse.   But I suffered, let that suffice me.
Suffice.   While we suffer for what we do not love
we love the one who doesn't love, and the rose is sterile.
And if a soul aspires there is no odor.   A perfume
shines on the pome, but always empty.

Marcel.

My solitude would not be yours.   Every brilliance
stays on the surface, and I fight in the dark
toward never, toward always.   I was deep darkness
that I hated on knowing it and on inhabiting my name.
My name, who knew it?   Name, complaints, words,
or better, that reflection of an eye that does not exist
because nobody looks at it, but it knows everyone.
That light fru-fru of clothing in the waltzes,

the numerous arms, but the same in the shadows
the blond hair, the dark, the waves,
the shells, like satin, like the wind in tulle,
everything crossed, and I heard it, while everyone was speaking.
Solitude, I never knew more than your impure name,
nor did I know other kisses that those that sound in it,
those that deep down continue resounding forever,
while you with your hand draw new shadows.

Swan.

I am knowing my profile.   But no: I mistrust.
If I admire a Botticelli, I know that pure colors
burn, but deceive.   If I listen to a sonata
I know that it strikes into the center, but it is never its music.
It is a dagger or a «theme» that incises the breast.
A «theme»;   that is life, with its impure word.

Marcel.

Once I told you: «Know,» and my image was
different and the same one that shines in you.
What I was not you were, but I have also been it.
For you I loved and in you I loved, while by myself I was lying.
I was what they used to be: implacable solitude.
World descending as if to deepen more.
As if the ruby were not uncorrupted blood
and the turquoise a sky that imitates other eyes.
But the more gold the poorer everything is, and it suffers.
That necklace I admire strangles me in my sleep.
The diadem is thorns, and the smile is blood.
And while I take leave, I gather up the shadows
that everything consists of, although they don't know it, and they lie lifeless.

Swan.

I knew it.   I lived?   I climbed the ladder
of that knowing.   But I thought how useless
it was to know it, and never.   But I did not lie.
A frock coat walked alone, with a glitter on its breast.
And behind?   Yes, inside, other glitters extinct.
Death takes on at times a beautiful frivolous face
that speaks to us and we don't hear: her fan is heard.
A lady, and we waltz, and we whirl: we sleep,
under mortal lights.

Marcel.

Now you are quiet, I know it.   Everything is silence, and it is enough.
In my room I am dying, with you all looking at me,
while I trace the last glimmerings of an orb.
Fugitive, instantaneous, but I desire no more.
I was and I have been.   Listen to me.

But no: I am my shadows.

SELECTED BIBLIOGRAPHY

Books of poetry by Vicente Aleixandre.

With the exception of the last two books, his poetic writing is included in *Obras Completas.* Madrid: Aguilar, 1968. The books listed below follow the order in which they were written. The year of publication is given in parenthesis.

Ambito (Ambit), 1924-1927. (1928)
Pasión de la tierra (Passion of the Earth), 1928-1929. (1935)
Espadas como labios (Swords like Lips), 1930-1931. (1932)
La Destrucción o el amor (Destruction or Love), 1932-1933. (1935)
Mundo a solas (World Alone), 1934-1936. (1950)
Sombra del paraíso (Shadow of Paradise), 1939-1943. (1944)
Nacimiento último (Ultimate Birth), 1927-1952, (1953)
Historia del corazón (History of the Heart), 1945-1953, (1954)
Picasso (Picasso), 1961, (1961)
En un vasto dominio (In a Vast Domain), 1958-1962 (1962)
Retratos con nombre (Portraits with Names), 1958-1965 (1965)
Poemas varios (Varied Poetry), 1927-1967 (1968)
Poemas de la consumación (Poemas of Consumation), 1968. Barcelona, Plaza Janés (1968).
Diálogos del conocimiento (Dialogues of Knowledge), 1969-1973. Barcelona, Plaza Janés (1974).

Studies of the Generation of 1927.

Alonso Dámaso. *Poetas españoles contemporáneos.* Tercera edición. Madrid: Editorial Gredos, S. A., 1965.
Cernuda, L. *Estudios sobre poesía española contemporánea.* Madrid: Ediciones Guadarrama, 1957.
Cirre, José F. *Forma y espíritu de una lírica española.* (1920-1935). México: Gráfica Panamericana, 1950.
Debicki, A. P. *Estudios sobre poesía española contemporánea:*

La generación de 1924-1925. Madrid: Editorial Gredos, S. A., 1968.

González Muela, J. *El lenguaje poético de la generación Guillén-Lorca.* Madrid: Insula, 1955.

Guillén, Jorge. *Lenguage and Poetry. Some Poets of Spain.* Cambridge, Mass., 1961.

Morris, C. B. *A Generation of Spanish Poets: 1920-1936.* Cambridge: Cambridge University Press, 1969.

Salinas Pedro. *Literatura española siglo XX.* Segunda edición. México: Antigua Librería Robredo, 1949.

Zardoya, Concha. *Poesía española contemporánea: Estudios temáticos y estilísticos.* Madrid: Ediciones Guadarrama, 1961.

Studies on the poetry of Vicente Aleixandre.

Bourne, Louis M. «The Spiritualization of Matter in the poetry of Vicente Aleixandre.» *Revista de Letras,* No. 22 (junio 1974), pp. 166-189.

Bousoño, Carlos. *La poesía de Vicente Aleixandre.* Madrid: Editorial Gredos, 1963.

Bousoño, Carlos. «The Greatness of Aleixandre's Poetry.» *Revista de Letras,* No. 22 (junio 1974), pp. 190-199.

Cabrera, Vicente. *Tres poetas a la luz de la metáfora: Salinas, Aleixandre y Guillén.* Madrid: Editorial Gredos, S. A., 1975.

Connell, Geoffrey. «'Posesión' and the Origins of Aleixandre's Cosmic Sensuality.» *Revista de Letras,* No. 22 (junio 1974), pp. 204-1209.

Durán, Manuel. «Vicente Aleixandre, Last of the Romantics: The 77 Nobel Prize for Literature.» *World Literature Today* (Spring 1978), pp. 204-208.

Ferrán Jaime. «Vicente Aleixandre—a half-century of poetry—1924-1974.» *Revista de Letras,* No. 22 (junio 1974), pp. 161-165.

Galbis, Ignacio R. «The Scope of 'Ambito': Aleixandre's First Cosmic Vision.» *Revista de Letras,* No. 22 (junio 1974), pp. 219-224.

Gimferrer, Pere. «La poesía última de Vicente Aleixandre.»

Plural, No. 32 (mayo 1974), pp. 23-27.

Jiménez, José Olivio. «Welcoming a New Book by Vicente Aleixandre: on 'Diálogos del Conocimiento' (1974).» *Revista de Letras,* No. 22, (junio 1974), pp. 253-262.

Luis, Leopoldo de. «Aleixandre: sus Diálogos del conocimiento.» *Cuadernos Hispanoamericanos,* No. 289-90 (julio-agosto 1974), pp. 314-325.

Puccini, Darío. «Hacia una tipología de la contradicción: Vicente Aleixandre: *Diálogos del conocimiento*». *Papeles de Son Armadans,* No. 81 (abril 1976), pp. 9-40.

Río, Angel del. «La poesía surrealista de Aleixandre.» *Revista Hispánica Moderna,* No. 2 (octubre 1935), pp. 21-23.

Schwartz, Kessel. *Vicente Aleixandre.* New York: Twayne Publishers, Inc., 1970.

Zardoya, Concha. «La técnica metafórica en la poesía española contemporánea. Vicente Aleixandre.» *Cuadernos Americanos,* No. 3 (mayo-junio 1961), pp. 275-277.

LIST OF POEMS IN TRANSLATION